The Church & Homosexuality
Searching for a Middle Ground

by Merton P. Strommen

Kirk House Publishers
Minneapolis, Minnesota

The Church and Homosexuality
Searching for a Middle Ground
by Merton P. Strommen

Library of Congress Cataloging-in-Publication Data
Strommen, Merton P., 1919
    The church and homosexuality : searching for a middle ground / by Merton P. Strommen.
        p. cm.
    Includes bibliographic references.
    ISBN 1-886513-17-1 (alk. paper)
        1. Homosexuality—Religious aspects—Lutheran Church. I. Title.
BX8074.H65 S87 2001
261.8'35766—dc21

                                                    2001029657

Kirk House Publishers, PO Box 390759, Minneapolis, MN 55439
Manufactured in the United States of America

Contents

ACKNOWLEDGMENTS

This book, which has been in development over a period of three years, has gone through a series of revisions. During this time I have profited from the review and reaction of people holding differing positions on the issue of homosexuality. These reviewers have included: psychologists, theologians, therapists of homosexuals, youth directors, bishops, pastors, homosexuals, lesbians, and parents. More than 65 people have given their reactions to this document while I have listened.

I wish to acknowledge, with special thanks, the insights and suggestions of these people. Their comments to versions of this manuscript have created for me a significant learning experience. A few of those listed below reject the basic premises of this book or contest certain points. Most, however, have affirmed what is written and offered helpful critiques and comments. All have been helpful in my personal odyssey of seeking to arrive at a position that squares with what I know from research, theology, and the Christian faith.

THEOLOGIANS: James Nestingen (professor, Luther Seminary, St. Paul), Roland Martinson (professor, Luther Seminary, St.Paul), Martin Synnes (Norwegian School of Theology, Oslo, Norway) John Christoperson (campus pastor, Boise, ID.), Walter Wink (professor, Auburn Theological Seminary, NY), Duane Olson (Luther Seminary, St. Paul).

BISHOPS: David Preus (bishop emeritus, The American Lutheran Church), Mark Hanson, (bishop, St. Paul Area Synod, ELCA), David Olson (bishop, Minneapolis Area Synod, ELCA), Peter Strommen (bishop, NorthEast Minnesota Synod, ELCA), Richard Foss (bishop, North Dakota Synod, ELCA)

PSYCHOLOGISTS: Roland Larson (counselor), Tom Kiresuk (professor, University of Minnesota Medical School), Joseph Nicolosi (clinical director, Thomas Aquinas Psychological Clinic).

MEDICAL DOCTORS: Tim Johnson (medical consultant), C. Everett Koop (former U.S. Surgeon General), Pat Cole (Hennepin County Medical Center); H. Mead Cavert (former faculty, University of Minnesota Medical School).

YOUTH DIRECTORS: Dick Hardel (Youth and Family Institute, Augsburg College), Tom Hunstad (Westwood Lutheran Church), Larry Johnson (Lutheran Youth Encounter), Richard Ross (Southwestern Baptist Theological Seminary), Paul Hill (Wartburg Theological Seminary), Karen Jones (Huntington College) Dave Rahn (Huntington College).

PASTORS: Erling Pettersen (director general, Church of Norway Council), Craig Lewis (senior pastor, Central Lutheran Church, Minneapolis), Harold Tollefson (retired) ,Bryce Eichlersmith (Oak Grove Lutheran Church, Minneapolis), Luther Strommen (retired), Morris Vaagenes (North Heights Lutheran Church, Minneapolis)

PROFESSIONALS: Al Quie (former governor, Minnesota), James Strommen (lawyer), David Moen (community youth leader), Lucy Hulme (teacher), Julie Christensen (counselor), Bruce Nicholson (Lutheran Brotherhood)

PARENTS and FRIENDS: Marilyn and Don Mueller, Richard and Cathy Jefferson, Ruth Cavert, Otto J. Reitz, Jack Swan, Jay Kershaw.

I appreciated the opportunity to dialog with and learn from these many people.

My special thanks also goes to editor Ron Klug, whose great skill has enhanced this manuscript by bringing greater clarity and readability to what I have tried to say.

PREFACE

This revised addition profits from a number of key books, articles, and interviews that have become available to me since the writing of my first edition. As a result I have added 16 pages of text.

I am grateful for the scholarly work of psychologists Stanton Jones and Mark Yarhouse. Quotations from their book, *Homosexuality: The Use of Scientific Research in the Church's Moral Debate* have been most helpful in strengthening the argument of this book.

Theologian Robert Gagnon's erudite Biblical scholarship adds another dimension to the theological debate. His book, *The Bible and Homosexual Practice,* contributes an important dimension to what I have written.

On the practical side, psychotherapist Richard Cohen's account of his journey to freedom from same-sex attractions provides valuable insight into what is needed for changing from homosexual practice to a heterosexual orientation.

Coinciding with the publication date of this edition is a very special journal article by psychologist Warren Throckmorton. He pioneers in supplying research information supportive of the hypothesis that sexual reorientation is possible for some. His article underscores how such change occurs primarily for those who are religiously motivated.

Adding to this edition are the stories I heard at one time from eight ex-gays as well as the stories I heard at another time from eight gays, six of whom are in committed relationships .These people whose stories were moving and provocative, gave me added insight into the struggles such people have in coping with same-sex attractions.

As can be assumed, a revision also provides the welcome opportunity to add, delete, and make minor corrections found in the first edition.

Merton Strommen, May 11, 2002

FOREWORD

I wish the reader could have seen the effort that went into producing the many revisions of this manuscript. If you wanted proof of this author's sincerity and authenticity in his pursuit of a balanced, informed, and healing solution, the evidence is here. I was impressed by the author's struggle and personal transformation as he kept his own moral compass but at the same time did all he could to be responsive and adapt his writings to accommodate the large number of reviewers and critics whose opinions he sought and respected.

I am Mert Strommen's friend of many years and his research colleague. I believe he asked me to be a reviewer because of my background in the practice of psychotherapy and in treatment outcome research. I was quite comfortable dealing with issues pertaining to the philosophy of science, the examination of the logic of arguments, and the quality of the evidence. However, perhaps like many of the readers of this book, I soon learned of the vast complexity of the topic of sexual identity and the Christian church, and the very strong feelings and fixed opinions that are so readily expressed by friends, family, and colleagues. There were many surprises for me.

I lacked full appreciation of the policy battles that are being waged in the professional organizations. This book describes in detail many of these historical events, the related strongly held beliefs, and the contentious manner in which they have been expressed. I was also impressed with how little I knew about the professional propaganda wars that are being waged. My only source of information was the chapter on sexuality which appeared in Kaplan and Saddock's *Comprehensive Textbook of Psychiatry*, seventh edition, not just the section on homosexuality, but the entire chapter on sexuality. Other than that, I was essentially asleep on these topics.

I was surprised at the vehemence with which several of my colleagues and friends objected to what they perceived was the "we—they" tone of arguments and presentations of the earlier revisions. I have a benign and positive background and experience with homosexuals and have a number of fine, productive, decent, caring, intelligent, and creative friends and colleagues. However, those objecting to even raising the distinction made it sound as though the book were recommending that there should be abbreviations after our names indicating our affiliations, i.e., Tom Kiresuk, PhD., HtS. (Doctor of Philosophy and Heterosexual). Mert Strommen has done everything possible to eradicate this potential impression, although individuals holding extreme views will probably never be satisfied.

I was taken aback by overgeneralizations that plague the discussions in this topic area. The term "some homosexuals" drifts into "homosexuals." The same is true for "heterosexuals" or "those Christians." In talking and reading about this topic, it is often unclear when the line is crossed from specific subclass taxonomy into universal inclusion. The author has studiously clarified his writing in this regard.

I was impressed at the naïve and simplistic dogma based on genetics at a time when the awe inspiring, magnificent complexity regarding the characteristics, function, interaction, and evolution of the human genome are being revealed to us daily. It is hard to believe that anyone would stake a claim for complex human characteristics and for moral determination on the basis of simple genetic arguments. Strommen has emphasized the genetic/environment interaction position.

I was also surprised at the frequency with which disputes involve the free use of causal attributions based on *post hoc ergo propter hoc* arguments in which one event is asserted to be the cause of a later event simply by virtue of having happened earlier. Reviewing my psychotherapy practice conducted in a hospital psychiatric service, I cannot recall any cases in which there were good and wholesome family backgrounds. Yet, it never occurred to me that these unfortunate circumstances caused their sexual preference of heterosexuality or homosexuality. If anything, these unfortunate circumstances contributed to unhappy and conflicted interpersonal behaviors whatever the sexual orientation. Strommen has strong prior beliefs regarding the influence of early experiences and supports these beliefs with his beliefs with evidence from several sources. A central theme of this book is the battle for young minds. Perhaps like many readers, I was unaware of this battle and am grateful to Strommen for bringing this to light.

I was surprised that the representatives on both sides of the argument tended to ascribe certainty and infallibility to the products of scientific research. Research scientists argue their points of view in a strong manner, bringing the best lines of information to support their claims. However, these are only hypotheses put forward in order to be examined, attacked, and superceded in an endless process of reasoning, intuiting, evidence gathering, and testing. The best scientists that I know continuously attack and test their own theories.

But let us put these beliefs in infallibility of science to a test. The problems associated with all treatment outcome research includes sample selection and sample size, treatment assignment and research design, research measures (specification of anticipated outcomes in terms of behavior, attitude, psychological and physical status, quality of life, relationships), methods of analysis, short and long-term follow-up, dealing with missing data (treatment drop-outs, self selection, missing follow-up data), conclusions and claims made from the findings. In terms of purely research answers, can we investigate nature's experiment? This is how you could do it. Clone hetero and homosexuals of various degrees of genetic predisposition, randomly assign them to families having various characteristics, controlling for the quantitative sexual predilections of the parents, and then controlling for the social, economic, and religious environments. With a large enough sample (just several million) this could be done. The findings would be of magnificent complexity but would not change the opinions of the major opponents in this dispute—not at all. They are appealing to moral authority and moral imperatives that by definition cannot and should not change. No research result could dissuade them. All research can be questioned.

The twist in my mind occurred when the arguments moved from disputes about what is (the nature and quality of evidence) to arguments about what should be. This was where we parted company, and I had no special expertise or knowledge to offer. Once again, I learned how much I had to learn. Upon self-examination, my social moral imperative turned out to be a naïve, primitive belief that people ought to treat each other in a decent manner and help each other out. After that, I had nothing to offer. Great theologians have nothing to fear from me.

There also were embarrassments for me. When talking to the younger generation (age 20 to 30) of friends and family regarding homosexual pornography as a cause of homosexuality, I think they regarded me as a naïve survivor of a simpler bygone era. Heterosexuals performing anal and oral sex can be observed 24 hours a day if one has a computer, modem, and telephone line. Some are self-advertised married couples who charge a minimal fee to observe them at their web sites. I realized that I had no special knowledge regarding the sexual activity of teenagers and young unmarried individuals. One colleague was especially adamant that the new computer age has totally changed the nature of communication worldwide, and that special interest groups can be and have been formed around all forms of sexuality.

My failure as a friend and colleague was as an inadequate detector of landmines scattered about in the manuscript. Some readers were incensed by statements whose bias and pejorative connotations were completely missed by me. Mert Strommen responded to each of these with great concern, soul searching, and self-examination. He contacted colleagues and sought reviews by experts. I was impressed with how concerned he was regarding his relationships with friends and colleagues in his pursuit of an equitable solution. Battle hardened authors that I know who are involved in controversial topic areas usually turn combative under criticism, stiffen their arguments, and counterattack. Mert Strommen has done everything he can to maintain communication and good will, keeping lines of communication open for negotiation and amicable solutions.

For me the most memorable aspect of this manuscript was the dramatic passage of the author through the landscape of strongly held beliefs and opinions, along with the conflicting lines of evidence, attempting to understand them all, and include them all in a constructive, loving solution. His beliefs are openly presented. They are as transparent as his intense effort to discover a loving, healing solution in which no one sacrifices their integrity or subordinates their deeply held beliefs.

Thomas J. Kiresuk, Ph.D.
Chief Clinical Psychologist, Hennepin County Medical Center
Professor of Clinical Psychology, University of Minnesota Medical School
Director, Center for Addiction and Alternative Medicine Research, Minneapolis Medical Research Foundation
Director, Program Evaluation Resource Center, Minneapolis Medical Research Foundation

INTRODUCTION

The issue of homosexuality wracks congregations and denominational judicatories, causing sharp divisions, emotionally charged exchanges, and much pain for homosexuals and their families. This polarization is intensified when people assume extreme positions at either end of the controversy.

At one end are those who offer homosexuals nothing but condemnation and rejection. Their goal is to drive homosexuals from the church as sinners who are an abomination to God.

At the other end are the supporters of what is called the militant gay agenda. In an unquestioning way they affirm that homosexuality in all its manifestations should be affirmed and celebrated.

I believe that there are good theological, psychological, and sociological reasons for avoiding the two extremes and searching for a middle ground. I believe that there are many pastors and lay leaders in Christian churches who are looking for an alternative to these polar opposites. And I believe that what is needed is a dialectical approach to ministry that avoids the two extremes and offers an intelligent, well-informed, compassionate response to the difficult questions surrounding homosexuality and the church.

I believe that the one extreme—the condemnation and rejection of homosexuals—can be dispensed with quickly by any Christian who believes the gospel of God is unmerited grace and forgiveness. We need to proclaim clearly that God loves homosexuals as much as he loves the rest of us—all of us sinful and broken, all of us redeemed and in the process of transformation.

This means that homosexuals should be welcomed in our churches. Homosexuals who accept the forgiveness found in Christ should be a part of our faith communities. This welcome and acceptance should be extended also to those who are convinced their sexual orientation is God's creation. The Bible calls us to such loving acceptance. Jesus says, "Love one another as I have loved you." It is impossible to imagine that Christ, while seated with tax collectors and sinners in the home of Levi, would have excluded homosexuals. We who confess each Sunday that we are sinful and unclean have no right to condemn or treat homosexuals harshly. We are brothers and sisters in Christ, members of the same body.

I believe that the other pole—what I have termed the militant gay agenda of unquestioning endorsement of homosexuality— needs a more thorough analysis. For some it has a special appeal in the way it tries to protect homosexuals from injustice. However, I believe that this position is built on assumptions that lack support.

Both extremes polarize people and tend to shut off intelligent discussion. As a result, there is a great deal of valuable information about homosexuality that is not being shared with the general public. One purpose of this book is to present this neglected information.

One of my convictions is that in a complex matter like homo- sexuality (as with issues of race or war and peace) we need to listen to all the best-informed voices, even those with whom we may not initially agree. In the chapters that follow I will present findings from the most careful research studies on homosexuality.

I write out of concern for homosexuals and their families. I have discovered that few, if any, initially wanted this orientation. Their discovery that they might be homosexual drew feelings of dismay, fear, and not a little anquish. To their discovery came the added pain, for some at least, of being ill-treated or outright con- demned by a few misinformed people. Especially painful for young homosexuals has been the task of telling their parents they are homosexuals.

I can understand why many homosexuals desperately want to establish their orientation to be as normal as left handedness; why they wish to be viewed as healthy and religiously acceptable as heterosexuals. I can understand why they want their orientation to be established as being equal to that of heterosexuals. As it is now, their orientation cuts them off from many aspects of life that heterosexuals enjoy.

I write as a Lutheran pastor, committed to the gospel, to the Scriptures and the tradition of the church, with more than 40 years experience in the ministry.

I have a new appreciation for the important role of the church—the faith conmmunity. Her mission is two-fold— to make disciples of all nations and to love one another as Christ has loved us. Stated another way—the mission of the church is to welcome everyone in the name of Christ and to transform lives in the name of Christ.

Transformation is at the heart of the church's redeeming message. The apostle Paul writes, "Do not be conformed to this world but be transformed by the renewal of your mind, that you may prove what is the will of God, what is good and acceptable and perfect" (Ro.12.2) There are many homosexuals whose lives make It very clear that they need to be transformed and many who wish they could be transformed.

The church must be one place where all people will feel welcomed and loved. It should be one place where homosexuals who are satisfied with their orientation can find fellowship and one place where those outside the kingdom or those dissatisfied with their orientation can be given help .Love needs to be sensitive to the needs of both groups.

I write also as a research psychologist with a doctorate in educational and clinical psychology. I am a life member of the American Psychological Association and hold Fellow Status in Division 36, Psychology of Religion. For more than 40 years I have developed and interpreted major research studies involving people of all denominations. The agency of which I was founder and president is Search Institute of Minneapolis.

I write, too, as one with a special concern for young people. Early in my ministry I became the part-time youth director of my denomination and campus pastor at Augsburg College. As part of my doctoral studies, I carried out a national study of Lutheran youth. Since then I have carried out a number of national studies about youth to help those who work with youth to more effectively minister to their needs. This same concern for youth motivates my writing of this book.

My goal is not to offer the final word on these highly complex issues, but to contribute to a realistic, informed, compassionate discussion about the issues surrounding homosexuality and the church.

— *Merton P. Strommen*

Chapter One

WHO ARE HOMOSEXUALS?

In order for us to have an intelligent, compassionate, balanced discussion about homosexuals, we need to understand who they are and how they have been viewed throughout history. A key to this understanding is to realize that not all homosexuals are alike. There is great variety within the area of homosexual feelings and behavior.

In order to see clearly we need to free ourselves of sweeping generalizations. This requires that we start not with our biases and prejudice—one way or another—but with the best psychological, sociological, and historical research currently available.

The discussion that follows is limited to literature about male homosexuality, because studies on homosexuality focus on males. Scientific information on lesbians is limited, although, in listening to the case histories of lesbians, I have noted strong similarities with male homosexuals.

The Variety of Homosexuals

According to the *Comprehensive Textbook for Psychiatry* published in the year 2000, sexual orientation refers to a person's erotic response tendency—homosexual, bisexual, or heterosexual—towards other persons of the same or other sexual orientation which consists of three components: desire, behavior, and identity. In a particular individual these three components may not be identical.

The term bisexuality refers to an erotic tendency, an individual identity, and sexual behavior. Although it has been portrayed by some as a transitional state in development to a heterosexual or gay or lesbian identity, it describes the sexual behavior and sexual orientation of many men and women at some point in their lives.

The acquisition of sexual identity is generally a developmental process that occurs over time. This process consists of stages.

The first is a period of growing awareness and/or confusion about same-sex erotic feelings. This is followed by a time when these feelings begin to have relevance to the person's life. The final stage is an extended phase of growing acceptance and pride in one's new identity.

It should be noted, however, that not all persons who experience homoerotic desire or participate in homosexual behavior develop a lesbian, gay, or bisexual identity.

The terms gay or straight are not absolute categories because there is a continuum between the two polarities of heterosexuality and homosexuality. A person can be halfway between these two polarities and classify as a bisexual. Or, one can be closer to either the heterosexual or homosexual pole (Sadock and Sadock, 2000).

Classifications

There are individual differences among homosexuals as is true for any classification of people. I have classified them into six informal groups recognizing that there may be considerable overlap in my classification

First are the deeply devout homosexuals who are loyal to their church and who want full acceptance and recognition. Many live in committed relationships and observe moral boundaries. Usually they maintain a low profile and are not featured in the media. Ideally, they should not identify themselves as homosexuals but as children of God, as believers in Jesus Christ who live out the life of Christ in the world.

Second, are non-church gays who live quietly with a partner and are less visible because they tend not to be involved in gay social activism. Many are doctors, lawyers, politicians, and others who contribute enormously to social good. Recently one such person was honored by the Minnesota state legislature for his many years of service as a legislator.

Third, are ardent gays dedicated to changing legislation (church, state, and federal) in the hope that a gay lifestyle will be accepted by the general public as normal This category includes persons from the other groups. I single them out for special consideration because they are the ones who are pressing for the ordination of practicing gays, the blessings of same-sex marriages, instruction in public schools regarding gay living, adoption rights for same-sex parents, and legal rights for committed partners.

Fourth, are closet gays who are living with a sense of guilt and shame over their homosexual behavior. They wish they could change but find they cannot. A classic illustration is the former president of the Association of Free Lutheran Churches (AFLC) whose secret involvement in homosexual activity eventually became public knowledge and resulted in his public confession of guilt.

Fifth, are promiscuous gays including those who favor gay sex in public places. In 1999, several gays published a book opposed to public decency laws. The book is entitled *Public Sex: Gay Space*. The authors claim that efforts to curtail all forms of gay-related sexual experience is repression forced on the gay community by outmoded right-wingers, paranoids, and religious fanatics. Another book, this one by Professor George Chauncey (1994) of the University of Chicago entitled, *Gay New York* gives a well-documented description of this gay lifestyle.

The sixth group consists of those who classify as the "leather" subculture of homosexuals. They follow bondage and sodomy rituals that eroticize pain, dominance, and humiliation. The deviant rape of 13-year-old Jesse Dirkhising by two gay "lovers" resulted in the boy's death, one that was as cruel and violent as the much publicized death of Matthew Shepard, a young gay man who was beaten, hung on a fence, and left to die. The death of Jesse Dirkhising gained little notice in the national press because it was not classified as a "hate crime" (La Barbera, 2000).

These are not precise groupings, but they illustrate the variation that exists in the homosexual community, a variation that must be recognized. Comments accurate for one group may not be accurate for another.

A formal classification is available from anthropologist Gilbert Herdt, based on his studies of ritualized homosexuality among the Sambia people in New Guinea and his review of anthropological studies of homosexual practices in other cultures. He has identified three types of sexual development—linear, sequential, and emergent—that occur cross-culturally and help to explain variations in patterns of sexual orientation.

Linear development refers to sexual behavior that occurs without significant change across a lifetime. *Sequential development* describes a developmental pattern that incorporates important change at different life stages (for example, males who practice homosexual behavior during childhood and are exclusively heterosexual as adults). *Emergent development* occurs in societies that allow some degree of ambiguity and uncertainty in adult sexual behavior (Stein, 2000).

Herdt also describes a typology of homosexuality based on the organization of same-sex sexual behavior cross-culturally. The first type is *age-structured homosexuality*, which usually involves sex between older males and younger males. This includes a sequential pattern of childhood same-sex practices that yields to primarily heterosexual behavior in adulthood.

Another form of homosexuality is *gender-reversed homosexuality*, which consists of a reversal in the normative sex-role dress and behavior. An example of this is the American Indian *berdache*.

A third type is *role-specialized homosexuality* in which same-sex activity is restricted to certain social roles and positions. An illustration Herdt gives is the American Indian *shamans* who cross-dress and engage in homosexual behavior.

Extent of Homosexuality

Herdt describes the *modern gay movement* as a fourth type of homosexual organization. He states that homosexuality in contemporary America is a new form of homosexual practice that comprises a sexual orientation, a social identity, and a political movement (Stein, 2000).

These classifications show the considerable variation in how homosexuality has been expressed in different periods of history and in different cultures. What we do not know is whether there has been variation in the percentage of people identifying themselves as homosexuals in different periods of history. Today the idea that ten percent of our population are homosexual or lesbian is widely accepted. As the following information will indicate, this is not true.

A research team at the University of Chicago, using the resources of its National Opinion Research Center (NORC), carried out a scientific study of the sexual practices of people in the United States. It is the only one of its kind. Using information from interviews of 3,432 randomly selected American men and women between the ages of 18 and 59, they were able to arrive at a reasonably accurate picture of the incidence and prevalence of sexual practices in 1994. When respondents were asked whether they consider themselves heterosexual, homosexual, or bisexual, 2.8 percent of the men identify themselves as homosexual and 1.4 percent of the women (Michael, et al. 1994).

Consistent with this study were two larger studies in France and England. The British survey conducted 18,876 face-to-face interviews with people aged 16 to 59, and the French study interviewed 20,055. Both studies identified only 1.1 percent as having had a same-gender sexual experience "in the past year" (Laumann et al. 1994).

The evidence is strong that the number who identify themselves as homosexuals is three percent or less.

There is considerable difference, however, in the percentage of homosexuals found in large cities as compared to rural areas. Note in the following table the contrast in percentages of homosexuals by place of residence. These statistics, reported in *The Social Organization of Sexuality: Sexual Practices in the United States* (Laumann, 1994, p.304), are also based on the only national scientific study of sexual behavior made in the United States, the one conducted by the National Opinion Research Center of the University of Chicago.

Table 1
Percentage Reporting Same-Gender Sex Partner the Past Year

Place of Residence	*Percentage*
Top 12 central cities (e.g. New York, Los Angeles, Chicago, San Francisco)	10.2 percent
Next 88 central cities	3.5 percent
Suburbs of top 12 cities	2.7 percent
Suburbs of next 88 cities	1.6 percent
Other urban areas	1.8 percent
Rural areas	1.0 percent
Average for total group	2.6 percent

The estimate of ten percent of the population being homosexual is accurate for those living in the 12 largest cities but incorrect when applied to those living in the suburbs, other urban areas, or rural areas.

Two factors may contribute to the disproportionate number of homosexuals in the 12 largest cities. One is the migration to cities by those who would distance themselves from the negative attitudes of friends, family, and church toward homosexuality. A second factor may be that large cities provide a more congenial environment for the expression of their same-gender sexuality.

Homosexuality In Early Societies

In the past, homosexuality has not posed the same issues as today. Known since the dawn of civilization and referred to often in Greek and Roman literature, homosexuality was not openly discussed until the nineteenth century. It was not until the end of the twentieth century that a gay liberation movement has emerged and made homosexuality a controversial issue.

John Boswell, professor of history, Yale University, provides a detailed confirmation of this fact in his comprehensive account of homosexuality in medieval Europe. Based on his ten-year study of documents in a dozen different languages, he concludes for that period that "neither Christian society nor Christian theology as a whole evinced or supported any particular hostility to homosexuality" (Boswell, p.333).

He notes in the introduction to his book that what he writes is "specifically intended to rebut the common idea that religious belief—Christian or other—has been the cause of intolerance in regard to gay people. Religious beliefs may cloak or incorporate intolerance, especially among adherents of revealed religions which specifically reject rationality as an ultimate criterion of judgment or tolerance as a major goal in human relations." (p.6).

He reports that early Christian writers were concerned over sexual exploitation of minors or incest resulting from slave trade. But not until 533 A.D. did any part of the Roman empire see legislation outlawing homosexual behavior, even though Christianity had been the state religion for more than two centuries (p.171). The Christian hierarchy in the seventh through tenth centuries considered homosexuality no more reprehensible than comparable heterosexual behavior (for example, extramarital sex) (p.179).

A more virulent hostility appeared in the popular literature of the last half of the twelfth century. Boswell closely relates this hostility to a general increase in intolerance toward minority groups (Jews, heretics, Muslims, proponents of witchcraft, etc.) during the thirteen and fourteen centuries.

In their studies of primitive societies, C.S. Ford and F. A. Beach found that 49 out of the 76 societies accepted homosexuality as normal (Ford and Beach, 1951). In some of these societies the practice was a part of initiatory rites for young men.

In New Guinea and outlying islands of Melanesia in the Pacific, homosexuality was an accepted part of everyday life. It was a cultural tradition of the Sambic tribe in New Guinea for males between the ages of nine and nineteen to live together and practice homosexual activity. When they married at the age of nineteen, their homosexual activity ceased (Money, 1988).

This acceptance of homosexuality as a normal, cultural tradition in primitive societies is in sharp contrast to the attitudes of many Africans. They evidence strong feelings against the practice. Their attitudes of shame in connection with any kind of extramarital sex is so strong that they are unwilling to acknowledge its possible role in the epidemic of AIDS that is devastating the continent. A heartrending article in the February issue of *Time* magazine (McGeary, 2001) describes the impact of AIDS in the southern countries of this continent and "the deep silence about their heterosexual activity that makes African leaders and societies want to deny the problem."

Greeks who accepted the bisexuality of men allowed for the institution of *paiderastia,* a word which is derived from *pais* ("a young man") and *(eran* "to love"). The relationship was a spiritual and sensual affection of an older man for a younger one, in which the young men were known as "sexual companions." It was a relationship that could not be called *pedophilia*, the sexual love of children. In fact, sexual relations with children was punished in Ancient Greece (Licht, 1925).

In ancient Rome, homosexuality was accepted as a natural and normal aspect of a man's sexual life. Homosexual practices were associated with the names of many emperors and many other Roman notables. For instance, Julius Caesar was ironically called "the husband of all women and the wife of all men." Other prominent men associated with bisexuality were Augustus, Tiberius, Domitian, Hadrian, and Trajan. Antinous was the well known lover of Hadrian (Kiefer, 1934).

Judaism and Homosexuality

In Old Testament times "unnatural sins" were thought to defile the land which belonged to the Lord. Among these sins was homosexual intercourse, a practice associated with the Canaanites. Sacred sodomy in the form of a temple prostitute was an imported Canaanite practice, believed to have been introduced into Judea at the time of the early kings (Epstein, 1948).

Though the book of I Kings does refer to male and female temple prostitutes being attached at times to the temple in Jerusalem, the repression of these practices among Jewish people was apparently quite effective. Writing about Judaism and sex in the two volume *Encyclopedia of Sexual Behavior*, Rabbi Samuel Glasner quotes the Talmud as indicating that homosexuality and bestiality were infrequently practiced among the Israelites (Glasner, 1961).

Orthodox Jews, who draw on a history of 3500 years and the writings of both the Hebrew Bible (Old Testament) and the Talmud, regard homosexuality as something to be avoided but not harshly condemned. It may be fair to say that they regarded the condemnation of homosexuals as a greater sin than the practice of homosexuality itself. Nevertheless, they join traditional Christians in interpreting Scripture as viewing homosexuality to be undesirable, not to be encouraged, something that is awry.

Emergence of the Gay Culture in America

If we skip in time to the 1890s we can take advantage of a detailed history of the gay culture written by a professor at the University of Chicago, George Chauncey, who has adopted the goal of writing a definitive history of homosexuality in our country. Having completed one book that brings the historical record up to the year 1940, *Gay New York* (1994), he is now involved in writing a second book that will give information up to the present time.

He writes about men who forged a distinctive culture with its own language and customs, its own traditions and folk histories, its own heroes and heroines. Some of these men were involved in long-term monogamous relationships they called marriages; others participated in an extensive sexual underground that by the beginning of the century included well-known cruising areas in the city's parks and streets, gay bathhouses, and saloons with back rooms where men met for sex.

Chauncey argues in his book that the classification of people as being either homosexual or heterosexual is a recent creation. Only in the 1930s, 1940s, and 1950s did this conventional division of men replace another classification, a division using the two words "fairies" and "normal" The word "fairy" was used because many homosexuals were seen as effeminate. The word "normal" was used to express a widely held judgment.

At this time laws in New York city criminalized not only the gay mens's sexual behavior but also their association with one another, their cultural styles, and their efforts to organize and speak on their own behalf. Hundreds of gay men were arrested in New York City every year in the 1920s and 1930s for cruising or visiting gay locales; thousands were arrested every year in the postwar decade. The medical judgment against them was that they were mentally ill and needed treatment. This judgment they fiercely resisted (Chauncey,1994).

Writers began to champion the cause of the gay culture. Edward Carpenter, an English poet and friend of Walt Whitman, glorified homosexuality as the truest, finest, highest form of love. He contended that the bonds of friendship between two males were more profound and faithful and meaningful than could exist under ordinary circumstances between man and woman (Cory, 1961).

Efforts were undertaken to prove that homosexuality is inborn. Studies were made in the hope of identifying possible physiological or anatomical differences or to see if hormonal differences caused homosexuality.

When did homosexuality become a major issue? Chauncey credits its beginning with the Stonewall rebellion that occurred June 26, 1969, when the police raided the Stonewall Inn, a bar frequented largely by homosexuals. This event, which resulted in a riot, marks the time when the gay culture became a political movement dedicated to the purpose of removing the stigma from homosexuality. This Stonewall rebellion took place at the time of student protests against the war in Viet Nam and the civil rights movement led by Dr. Martin Luther King, Jr. This included the Poor People's Campaign with a mule train, Southern violence, racial riots following King's assassination, and militant efforts to gain voting rights for blacks.

The Gay Activist Movement

Today the goal of the gay activist movement is to identify homosexuality as an acceptable, normal, and safe way of life. Its advocates demand that society view homosexuality as a sexual preference on equal footing with heterosexuality. To quote Suzanne Pharr, one of their spokespersons:

> We want the elimination of homophobia. We are seeking equality. Equality that is more than tolerance, compassion, understanding, acceptance, benevolence, for these still come from a place of implied superiority, favors granted to the less fortunate. . . .The elimination of homophobia requires that homosexual identity be viewed as viable and legitimate and as normal as heterosexual identity. It does not require tolerance; it requires equal footing (Pharr, 1988).

The gay movement argues its case with the same language that has stricken the nation's conscience on racial justice, labeling objections to its arguments as "hatred," "bigotry," and "intolerance." Its representatives present themselves as an oppressed group of people, and they identify their situation as comparable to what African-Americans have been enduring.

One of the first objectives of the gay activists was to remove the negative medical judgment found in the *Diagnostic and Statistical Manual* of the American Psychiatric Association which identified homosexuality as a psychiatric disorder. The medical judgment reaffirmed in 1963 was this: "The homosexual is an emotionally disturbed individual who has not acquired the normal capacity to develop satisfying heterosexual relations" (Socarides, 1992).

Gay activists called attention to a study by research psychologist Evelyn Hooker in which she compared the profiles of 30 homosexual men with 30 heterosexual men. Her comparison failed to show that homosexuals are more emotionally disturbed than heterosexual males.

Gay activists exerted political pressure on the American Psychiatric Association Committee on Nomenclature to change the description of homosexual behavior as an emotional disorder. The committee spearheaded a series of events that led to a decision made in 1973 to strike homosexuality from the list of psychiatric illnesses.

The pressures to remove homosexuality from the *Diagnostic and Statistical Manual of Psychiatry* were motivated by two issues. First was the hope that removing the stigma of sickness attributed to homosexual people would eliminate social discrimination. Second was the psychiatric profession's inability to identify with certainty the psychodynamic causes of homosexuality and the treatment that should follow (Nicolosi, 1997).

Today the agenda of militant gay activists is to establish homosexuality as being:

1. An innate, genetically determined aspect of the human body

2. Irreversible, something that cannot be changed.

3. Normal, as left-handedness is normal.

These three propositions undergird a widespread effort to gain acceptance for homosexuality. Their advocates contend that the historical condemnation of homosexuality by the Jewish and

Christian faiths is based on ignorance. They argue that scientific discoveries have advanced toward an ever-greater appreciation of the strength of nature, of innate biology.

An important voice for a biological point of view is John Money, Professor of Medical Psychology at Johns Hopkins University and Hospital. He has been much involved in psycho-hormonal research and has written 62 articles and books on sex. In his book, *Gay, Straight and In-Between* (1988) he presents his conviction that homosexuality is something that happens to a person. It is no more a preference than being heterosexual. It is something that is determined before birth.

However, he does admit that there is no evidence that prenatal hormonalization alone, independent of postnatal history, preordains a homosexual orientation. He contends that postnatal determinants enter the brain and influence the development. Though not able to establish his position scientifically, he theorizes that the effect of these cultural influences is predetermined by what has been established in the brain before birth (Money 1988).

Today gay activists are aggressive in their efforts to establish homosexuality as a gift of creation, as a normal part of life that can and should be celebrated. They use the term "homophobic" to describe anyone that values heterosexuality as superior to and "more natural" than homosexuality (Morin, 1977). Their use of the term means that most parents are homophobic because most parents do not want their child to grow up homosexual.

I can understand the motivation behind this effort to change attitudes toward homosexuality. I cringe at some of the horrible things which have been said and done to homosexuals—many of them by people who claim they are representing the Christian faith. What they do and say is an offense to the gospel. Their harsh judgments and attitudes of hatred are something to be eliminated.

At the same time there are sound theological, psychological, and sociological reasons for questioning the position of gay activists. Let us begin by looking at the best research on the causes of homosexuality.

Chapter Two

WHAT CAUSES HOMOSEXUALITY?

Do people simply choose to be homosexual? The answer for nearly all homosexuals is "no." Eric Marcus, a homosexual, has written a book entitled, *Is It a Choice?* In it he tells how for himself and others the dawning realization that one is a homosexual is both frightening and unwelcome.

At a conference at Central Lutheran Church in Minneapolis I listened to a research report based on interviews of 35 gays and lesbians who are or have been serving as Evangelical Lutheran Church in America (ELCA) clergy. For almost all of these people, coming to understand themselves as gay or lesbian was a gradual process, fraught with guilt, shame, confusion, danger, loneliness, and loss. Half of them had graduated from seminary before they fully realized they were gays or lesbians.

What then causes this homosexual orientation?

Stanton Jones and Mark Yarhouse, both psychologists, seek an answer to this question in their comprehensive review of research in *their* book, *Homosexuality: The Use of Scientific Research in the Church's Moral Debate.* They note that the origins of homosexuality are not clearly understood by scientists and the subject remains a subject of hot debate.(p.52)

The two men review research studies supporting a variety of theories: a psychoanalytic theory, Exotic Becomes Erotic theory, biological theories (prenatal hormonal hypothesis, gender nonconformity in childhood, anatomical brain structures) and also genetic hypotheses. They conclude that "no research to date provides ample support for any theory to the exclusion of another" (p.84). By this they mean "the scientific evidence about causation is simply inconclusive at this time." For that reason they favor an "interactionist hypothesis" where various psychological, environmental , and biological factors, together with human choice, are seen as contributing in differing degrees.

The four domains to which they refer cover a broad array of influences.

The first domain, that of biological antecedents, may include genetic and prenatal hormonal influences. The second domain, that of childhood experiences, could include childhood sexual trauma, gender atypical play, and poor parental relationships. The third domain, that of environmental influences, can include peer group influences, same-sex behavior, use of pornography, and subculture disinhibition. The fourth domain, that of adult experiences, can include willful or purposeful experimentation with same-sex behavior and subculture disinhibition. (pp.84-86). The contributing factor of personal choice is highly significant for adults. There is a significant percentage who indicate that homosexuality is their choice.

The authors note that each individual who later identifies as a gay or lesbian will have unique predispositions and experiences that are weighted differently for each individual. (Jones, Stanton & Mark Yarhouse, 2000)

Jeffrey Satinover, a former Fellow in Psychiatry and Child Psychiatry at Yale University gives this answer. He has practiced psychoanalysis and psychiatry with homosexuals for more than 20 years. Here is what he says when defining homosexuality as developmental:

> Like all behavioral and mental states, homosexuality is multifactorial. It is neither biological nor exclusively psychological, but results from an as-yet-difficult-to-quantify mixture of genetic factors, intrauterine influences, postnatal environment (e.g., parental, sibling, and cultural behavior), and a complex series of repeatedly reinforced choices occurring at critical phases in development (Satinover 1996).

In the American Psychological Association's pamphlet, *Answers to Your Questions about Sexual Orientation and Homosexuality*, is this quote: "Many scientists share the view that sexual orientation is shaped for most people at an early age through complex interactions of biological, psychological, and social factors."

Are Some People Born a Homosexual?

Many believe that science has proven that homosexuality is genetically determined, that homosexuals are born that way.

The two authors, Jones and Yarhouse, in addressing this question note that attention in the research field has shifted from psychological theories (though not refuted) to a focus on genetic and prenatal hormonal hypotheses. Though they find an impressive amount of research in support of these hypotheses (notably the much publicized initial findings of Bailey and Pillard, 1991), the findings have proven to be inconclusive.

Bailey who was the author with Pillard of an influential twins study on homosexuality, replicated his study using an improved sample (a random sample from the Twin Registry of Australia). The result of this study was unexpected. Evidence formerly giving support for a genetic causation of homosexuality had largely vanished. This carefully designed replication cast doubt on the significance of genetics in the causation of homosexuality (J. Michael Bailey, Michael P. Dunne and Nicholas G. Martin, 2000)

Behavioral geneticists find no evidence for this widely held belief that homosexuality is genetically determined. No research is able to do more than identify what seems to be a genetic predisposition toward homosexuality.

One research project by Dean Hamer in 1993 did seem to indicate that many gay men shared a common genetic marker in the x chromosome. This finding was hailed as a momentous scientific discovery—one that would help society transcend bigotry, heal family wounds, and lay to rest the nagging question. But this highly publicized study did not actually establish that a homosexual sexual orientation is determined by a specific gene.

Six years later the gene was yet to be found and interest in "gay gene" research waned among activists and scientists alike. Ruth Hubbard, professor emeritus at Harvard University and board member of The Council for Responsible Genetics, had this to say: "Searching for the 'gay gene' is not even a worthwhile pursuit. I don't think there is any single gene that governs complex human behavior. There are genetic components in everything we do. It is foolish to say genes are not involved, but I don't think they are decisive" (Brelis, 1999).

William Byne and Bruce Parsons (1999) from Columbia University reviewed 135 research studies, prior reviews, academic summaries, and chapters of books to see if they could substantiate a biological theory for homosexuality. They concluded that "not only is there little convincing evidence for a biological explanation of homosexuality, but there is little high-quality scientific research for any explanation."

Today's most respected researchers say only that genetics may contribute a predisposition to a homosexual orientation. They generally agree that homosexuality—like most other psychological conditions—is due to a combination of social, biological, and psychological factors. Homosexuality is developmentally determined. This point of view is reiterated by Simon LeVay, the researcher who made world-wide news after apparently discovering a difference in the brains of some homosexuals. The conclusion given in his book, *Queer Science,* is this:

> At this point, the most widely held opinion [on the causation of homosexuality] is that multiple factors play a role (LeVay, 1996).

When "gay gene" researcher Dr. Dean Hamer (himself a gay man) was asked if homosexuality was rooted solely in biology, he replied: "Absolutely not. From twin studies we already know that half or more of the variability in sexual orientation is not inherited." Environment can account for some or even most of the remaining variance.

Added confirmation to the fact that one is not born a homosexual comes in a new study, reported in 1999, that attempted to replicate the famed 1993 Hamer "gay gene" study. It failed to find a connection between male homosexuality and Xq28, the chromosomal segment which is suppose to be relevant. A May 10, 1999, article in *Science* reports on this study, "Male Homosexuality: Absence of Linkage to Microsatellite Markers at Xq28." One of the four researchers, Neil Risch (others were George Rice, Carol Anderson, and George Ebers), told the *New York Times* that he didn't believe the evidence for an x-linked gene had been very strong to begin with.

What Might be a Predisposing Genetic Factor?

A correlation has been observed between homosexuality and nonmasculine behaviors in boyhood. There seems to be a genetic predisposition toward certain characteristics we associate with effeminacy—a greater-than average tendency to anxiety, shyness, sensitivity, intelligence, and aesthetic abilities. It should be noted, however, that a correlation does not assume causation. The fact that these characteristics exist does not mean that they cause homosexuality.

In three studies, Hockenberry and Billingham (1987) found that an absence of what are considered masculine behaviors in boyhood is an even stronger predictor of homosexuality than the presence of feminine traits. A. J. Harry in a very large study— 1400 homosexuals and 280 heterosexuals—found that significantly more homosexuals recalled being labelled "sissy," being social loners, and wanting to be with girls. Through his study of 206 homosexuals, F. L. Whitham (1977) concluded that the greater the number of childhood indicators, the stronger the homosexual orientation in adulthood.

Those labelled "sissy," the loners, and those who preferred the company of girls, tend to shy away from rough boy activities and competitive games. This is a loss, because the early years of a boy help shape his concept of himself as a male. These studies indicate that boys in groups actualize the masculine potential in each other. Males in groups teach each other a resilience and trust that the "prehomosexual" boy misses.

Though these physiological factors may predispose a person toward a weak gender identification and consequent homosexuality, one cannot say that they predetermine homosexuality (Nicolosi, 1997). But to what degree might physiological factors incline a person towards homosexuality?

Two scientists from New Zealand, Neil E.Whitehead and Briar K. Whitehead, through their studies on intersexes, twins, and gene linkage come to the conclusion that the genetic contribution is approximately ten percent. In their book, *My Genes Made Me Do It! A Scientific Look at Sexual Orientation* (Whitehead, 1999), they contend that on average, ten percent of the influence on them to become homosexual is genetic.

They also indicate that society can emphasize or de-emphasize the genetic contribution by acting upon it or suppressing it. In other words, society and individuals can cultivate a genetic tendency towards any behavior or bring an opposite environmental factor to bear, thus changing the relative strength of the genetic factor. If a society encourages homosexuality, then the comparative influence of environment increases, and the genetic influence of ten percent drops even lower. An illustration of an environmental influence would be sexual abuse by older boys.

With onset of puberty, most boys between ages 8 and 14 experience a homosexual period. Unfortunately there are adolescent boys whose parents are ready to label them homosexuals when the boys report having homosexual feelings. What these parents do not know is that the vast majority of youngsters who engage in homosexual practices outgrow them.

This is an important point that I will pursue later. It relates to the high vulnerability of adolescent males who, when they admit to having homosexual inclinations, may be counseled to join a gay club at school. They may be told wrongly that they are homosexuals and that they should learn to live with this fact. This simply strengthens the homosexual inclination.

A Minnesota study by Remafedi, Resnick, Blum and Harris (1992) queried 34,706 students. They found that 26 percent of the 12-year-olds reported being "unsure whether they were gay or straight." This high percentage represents strong evidence of the sexual-identity confusion that is common to middle adolescent years.

Information such as this gives ample reason for not classifying teenage youth as gay simply because they report having such feelings. Doing so would be the same as classifying all males of the Sambic tribe in New Guinea as homosexuals because they traditionally are involved in homosexual practices until age 19, after which they marry.

Troublesome Theories About the Parental Factor

Authors Jones and Yarhouse report that among psychological theories, the psychoanalytic theory has been the most prominent theory of homosexuality. They note that the "classic" psychoanalytic theory of the "cause" of male homosexuality implicates a close-binding mother and a rejecting, absent, or detached father. The basic idea is that male homosexuality is caused by the failure of normal development of a secure male identity (Jones & Yarhouse, 2000)

The idea that parents contribute to the formation of homosexuality is sharply opposed by gays and those favorable to their point of view. They claim that the idea that homosexuality is caused by a weak or abusive father–son relationship theory has been discredited. Theologian Walter Wink said in a letter to me, "You should know better than to fall into the 'fathers are the cause' trap. We already went through the 'mothers are the cause' nonsense. Virtually all fathers in American society are distant— they no longer work in fields, come in for lunch, sit around the fire and tell stories."

True, there are many distant, unloving fathers and their effects on sons show up not only with homosexuals but also with those being counseled for other reasons. The case can be made that unloving or controlling parents are a factor in most cases of psycho-therapy. But to discount the theory of parental impact ignores the results of careful studies involving significant samples.

"Seymour Fischer and Roger Greenberg have had a continu-ing interest in finding out how well Freud's major ideas stand up to scientific appraisal. In 1977 they completed their first publica-tion *the Scientific Credibility of Freud's Theories and Therapy* which presented their first systematic attempt to ascertain the sound-ness of Freud's formulations.

Freud had conceptualized the development of homosexuality in the male as resulting from flawed Oedipal relationships, namely, too much closeness to mother and too much distance from father. In 1989, Fischer identified 58 empirical studies in the total literature concerned with parents of homosexuals. He analyzed the 58 studies and reported that a large majority supported the notion that homosexual sons perceive their fathers as negative, distant, unfriendly figures. However, only a minority of the studies supported the concept that homosexual men perceive their mothers as unusually close and seductive. Some of these studies were of unusually high quality in which a number of confounding variables were well controlled. The results of these studies also, supported the "negative father hypothesis".

One can conclude that the actual empirical data, as reported by Fischer supports the notion of a negative, distant father, but not the overly close mother. This represents validation for one important element of Freud's theory of homosexuality but lacks verification for another major component, namely, the impact of a close mother. (Fischer & Greenberg, 1996, p.137-138)

Cross cultural studies concerned with homosexuality have added additional support for this hypothesis. An analysis of coded data from anthropological observations of 186 societies showed that the frequency of homosexuality was linked to the amount of competition and hostility among male members. It should be noted that these are correlational studies and hence do not establish causation, namely, that distant fathers cause homosexuality. But it does allow for that possibility.

In his book, *Love Undetectable: Notes on Friendship, Sex and Survival,* Andrew Sullivan, a gay activist and author, says that any "honest homosexual" who ponders his family background from the perspective of the classic "distant father, overclose mother" theory will have to admit that Freud had something perceptive to say. In fact, Sullivan says, it would be self-deception to think of homosexuality as genetically inherited.

Those who counsel homosexuals find that their clients consistently single out their relationship to mother or father as a contributor to their homosexuality. Though it may not be a contributing factor for some, it has been found to be a prominent one for most homosexuals. Joseph Nicolosi, who had counseled over 1000 homosexuals during a 25-year period, concludes that "homosexuality, a developmental problem, is almost always the result of problems in family relations, particularly between father and son" (Nicolosi, 1997).

A warning is important here. Nicolosi's sample of homosexuals is limited to those who are dissatisfied with their orientation. It does not include those who are satisfied with their orientation and hence have not come for counseling. It is possible that many of these would report ideal home situations and insist that for them the parental factor does not apply.

Irving Bieber (1987) who interviewed more than1000 homosexuals in psychoanalytically focused interviews found mother and father relationships to be highly significant. He reports that 80 percent of the mothers in the homosexual sample were overly close to their son, spent a great deal of time with him, and preferred him to his siblings.

Contrastingly, when father–son relationships show an absence of loving, warm, constructive attitudes and behavior, homosexuality often occurs.

A few years later, Roy Evans replicated Bieber's work with similar results. The major improvement that Evans made over Bieber's study was that the findings he reported were based on the self-report of homosexuals who had never sought therapy (Roy Evans, 1969)

An illustration can be found in the family life of Olympic diver Greg Louganis. In his autobiography, *Breaking the Surface,*

Louganis (1995) tells of how his father terrorized the family. Teased by his male peers, Louganis developed an intense relationship with his mother who became his best friend and "soul mate." He tells that what he longed for and missed was intimacy and affirmation from men. This desire which became a romantic attraction, turned homosexual.

There is an undeniable connection for many homosexuals between poor quality of family relations and the emergence of homosexuality. A. Ibrahim (1976) links homosexuality with broken homes, unhappy childhoods, and poor relationships with both parents. Another therapist, W. E. Consiglio, asserts that one can assume there is a "focal family member" in the life of a homosexual client. This family member must be identified and worked with, directly or indirectly, in order to facilitate growth (Consiglio, 1994).

Another contributing factor, one rooted in a father-son relationship, and usually overlooked, relates to the son's misinterpretation of the reason for a father's absence from his life. The father may be a person whose church and/or work responsibilities have prevented him from giving much time to his son or demonstrating an adequate interest in his activities. The father may be a loving, devout churchman but the commitments he has taken on have made it almost impossible to give his son the time and interest he wants and needs.

Such a dynamic became apparent to me in a conversation I had with a friend of mine. His son who came to believe he might be gay (though not practicing homosexuality), sought counseling when away from home in a large city. After two years of therapy he was free from same-sex attractions, and understodd why he had expereienced them. He had discovered what it was that had contributed significantly to his homosexual development. It was his dad.

He had interpreted his father's lack of time for him as disinterest in him as a person and as a result had erected an emotional wall that severed meaningful relationships between the two of them.

I asked the father, "Were you aware of this?

He answered: "Not really. I noticed that his attitude towards me at times was surly and non-communicative. But I was too preoccupied to notice much else. Counseling at this time regarding our relationship would have been helpful."

"I was working full time and serving as president of our congregation. For me to get everything done, I had to have early breakfast meetings, late night meetings, Sunday meetings, and the like. I realize now that I was just too busy to notice him or give him time he wanted I had no idea that my absence from the family was hurting my youngest son."

What brought us together was a telephone call in which he haltingly and painfully asked:" Dad, will you forgive me"? His son is now happily married with a lovely family.

Here is a case where the primary cause of the son's homosexuality is not as much the absence of the father as it is the boy's defensive detachment from his father. The boy first misinterprets and concluded rejection from his dad. Then he self-protects by creating an emotional wall around his heart. Thus the father unwittingly contributes to a quiet rupture that prevents his son from identifying with his father's male role.

The father finished the conversation with these words: "Had he been told , 'God made you that way," I don't even want to think of the consequesces."

The Factors of Sexual Abuse and Erotic Fantasies

Another developmental factor is the sexual stimulation provided by older persons, friends, literature, or films. One especially significant environmental factor is sexual molestation by an older person, an experience common to many homosexuals. In Nicolosi,Byrd and Potts (1998) study of 882 dissatisfied homosexually-oriented people, the average age of the respondent's first homosexual contact with another person was 11 years. The average age of the one making the contact was 17 years.

D. Finkelhor (1984) found that boys victimized by older men were four times more likely to be currently involved in homosexuality than non-victims. In fact his study and that of Johnson and Shrier (1987) provide strong evidence that many preadolescent boys who were not developing as homosexuals became homosexuals because of sexual abuse. In other words, those who were developing heterosexually at the time of molestation turned out to be homosexual later in life. The strength of these two studies is found in the fact that comparison groups of non-molested boys were used.

In his book, Olympian Greg Louganis describes his relationship with a pedophile he met on the beach. He admits that he felt uncomfortable about their age difference, but in a certain way the experience felt right. He writes, "I kept going back for the affection, the holding, the cuddling—more than the sex. I was starved for affection" (Louganis, 1995).

Still another factor includes a person's willing preoccupation with erotic fantasies, his fixation on pornographic literature, or his involvement in guilt-creating sexual activities. This may be one time in the life of a homosexual that choice or volition is involved. It is significant that Mel White, a pastor and militant gay, acknowledged to Christian college students (2000) that pornographic literature was a part of his reading.

The discovery of gay pornography by a young adolescent can have a very habituating influence on the sexually confused and impressionable boy. As one psychiatrist explains:

Once imbedded, sexual fantasy cannot be erased. . . . habits linked to drive-related pleasures often overcome the will. In short order unregulated sexual tendencies become habits, then compulsions, and finally something barely distinguishable from addictions (Satinover, 1996).

As such behaviors are recorded in the brain, they gain increasing control over a person's thoughts. The older the person, the more fixed his orientation and the more difficult it is to change (Satinover, 1996). This effect, of course, would also apply for heterosexuals.

I listened for two and one-half hours one night as eight ex-gays (four men and four women) told their stories to two pastors who had publicly declared their disbelief that homosexuals can change. It was a sacred evening as these people told of their pain, their struggles, their release, and their joy over the new life given to them through the power of Christ's redemption. These people reflected a keen awareness of the factors that had contributed to their same-sex attractions—the roots which fostered and nurtured their erotic desires.

One woman spoke of having been sexually abused by family members during her years 8 to 12. Then at 16 years of age she was sexually abused by a pastor. During her high school years she became sexually promiscuous. A turning point for her was sitting in a gay bar and having a 50 year old woman "make a pass at her"—much to the amusement of those around her. The very thought that she might be like that when 50 years of age motivated her to seek help.

A second person identified himself as one who had the classic indicators of homosexuality when a boy. He grew up in a family of athletes where he was the uncoordinated one, the short, unattractive, shy, music loving, person who was taunted by classmates and criticized by his dad. But when he entered a gay bar, he was told by the men that he was handsome, attractive, and desireable. This was exciting to him.and the beginning of a life of promiscuity that lasted for 20 years.

Another told of a divorce that fractured his home and how he, a young boy, tried to become the support his mother needed. Later he came to see that two major roots contributing to his homosexuality were his preoccupation with pornographic literature and an unnatural attachment to his mother.

An African-American woman described her childhood as having been completely loveless—father gone and mother a traveling soloist. The only time she could remember ever being hugged by her mother was when she,a grown woman, had just experienced a tragedy. She entered a life of promiscuity that included both men and women and came to know the gay life

Another, now a pastor, told of being raised in the church and being serious about its teachings. As a seven year old boy he mistakenly thought that adultery involved only women and that sexual activity with other boys was okay. As result he became involved in same-sex activity throughout his elementary and high school years. Wanting to leave his homosexual practices, he chose a Bible college thinking that he would be safe and no longer be tempted by any gays. Not so. Then he entered seminary thinking that he would be safe there. Not so. Not until he was serving as a pastor and his involvement with other men became evident that he found the help he had been wanting.

Every one of these eight persons who told their stories that night reflected an awareness of a wide variety of precipitating factors in their homosexual attractions—ones that became evident to them through counseling. Each person.identified a constellation of factors that were deeply embedded as roots— ones that needed to be identified and severed. The causes of their same-sex attractions were indeed varied.

Psychotherapist Richard Cohen tells a similar story in his book *Coming Out Straight: Understanding and Healing Homosexuality.*He was sexually abused as a boy by his uncle and the recipient of disapproval and distance from his father. He experienced constant fighting and tears in his household and ,from early infancy, a love-hate relationship with his mother.

While in college, his lover introduced him to the New Testament and the person of Jesus Christ. He, a Jew, entered upon a spiritual quest that ended with him becoming a devout Christian. His subsequent spiritual journey and efforts to leave homosexuality are recounted in his book. Not until he was thirty years of age did he find the transformation he wanted.

Today, serving as a psychotherapist , Cohen is determined to help people who are struggling with the same issues that plagued him,He does this through *The International Healing Foundation* which he founded. He claims to have helped thousands of men, women, and adolescent make the transition from homosexuality to heterosexuality.The stories of six of his clients are included in the book.

Cohen identifies four stages that are usually involved in the recovery process he conducts. The four stages are these.

Stage One. The individual needs to cut ties with homosexual fantasy, stop homosexual behavior, terminate relationships with friends in the homosexual community, and build a support network of healthy love. He needs to build a sense of self-worth by developing a personal relationship with God.

Stage Two. The individual needs to develop skills for creating happiness in his present life. This involves cognitive therapy, developing communication and problem–solving skills, assertiveness training, and correcting faulty thinking. Here the client begins learning about feelings and needs.

Stage Three. The individual seeks to identify the homo-emotional wounds, heal them, and then fulfill them in healthy, nonerotic same-sex relationships. This is the pschodynamic work of recovery, exposing the wounds, grieving the pains, and losses of the past, learning to forgive, and finally moving on.

Stage Four. The individual now needs to identify hetero-emotional wounds, heal them, and then fulfill them in healthy opposite-sex relationships. He needs to learn about women from a man's perspective. (Cohen, 2001,p.108-109)

When asked how long is required for such therapy, Cohen indicated that it ranges from one to three years depending on the person's situation. When the 882 respondents in the study by Nicolosi, Byrd and Potts were asked how long they were involved in therapy, their average response was close to three and one-half years. Clearly, the relearning process is not a quick fix.

But Cohen is convinced that "What was learned can be unlearned. Let us embrace these beautiful sensitive souls. Let us love them into life." (Cohen 2001, p. 248)

Summary

As we have seen, the answer to the question,"What Causes Homosexuality?" is exceedingly complex and involves many factors. Seldom is a homosexual orientation a free choice. Usually it involves factors the homosexual did not choose. As research studies show, it is an oversimplification to say that people are born homosexual. There may indeed be a genetic predisposition, but other developmental and environmental factors play a more decisive role.

Chapter Three

SHOULD HOMOSEXUALITY BE CONSIDERED NORMAL?

As we have seen, part of what I have called the gay agenda is the contention that homosexual behavior is perfectly normal, as normal as heterosexuality. We now need to examine that assumption by looking at the evidence on all sides of this complex and troublesome question. We start by recognizing that the scientific and therapeutic communities are sharply divided on this question. Today psychologists and psychiatrists sharply disagree as to whether homosexuality should be regarded normal behavior.

Dr. Robert Spitzer, chairperson of the committee that made the 1973 decision to remove homosexuality from the list of psychiatric illness, says that removing homosexuality does not mean that homosexuality is normal or represents optimal functioning (Spitzer, 1973). The criteria he used in 1973 for determining what is a mental disorder were these: 1) experience of subjective distress; and 2) generalized impairment in social effectiveness or functioning. He concluded that homosexuality did not meet these two criteria. However, he did say in an interview with Dr. Laura Schlessinger, January 21, 2000, that for the homosexual "there is something not working" (Nicolosi, 2000).

Kaplan and Sadock's Comprehensive Textbook of Psychiatry points up the current disagreement among psychiatrists in the section on homosexuality. Here the author, Terry Stein, identifies homosexuality as "one of the most contentious issues within psychiatry during the latter part of the twentieth century" (Sadock and Sadock, 2000).

One reason is that some believe that the decision made in 1973 was a political decision and not a scientific one. R.Bayer (1981) in his book, *Homosexuality and American Psychiatry:The Politics of Diagnosis*, comments on the decision:

The result of the decision of 1973 was not a conclusion based upon an approximation of scientific truth as
dictated by reason, but was instead an action demanded
by the ideological temper of the times (Bayer, 1981).

The following is an eyewitness account of how this decision
was made, one which shows that a few determined gay activists
were successful in precipitating the decision of 1973.

"On May 3, 1971, the protesting psychiatrists broke into a
meeting of distinquished members of the profession. They
grabbed the microphone and turned it over to an outside activist,
who declared:

"Psychiatry is the enemy incarnate. Psychiatry has waged a
relentless war of extermination against us. You may take this as a
declaration of war against you . . . We're rejecting you all as our
owners"

"No one raised an objection. The activists then secured an
appearance before the APA's Committee on Nomenclature. Its
chairman allowed that perhaps homosexual behavior was not a
sign of psychiatric disorder, and that the Diagnostic and
Statistical Manual (DSM) should probably therefore reflect this
new understanding."

"When the committee met formally to consider the issue in
1973 the outcome had already been arranged behind closed
doors. No new data was introduced, and objectors were given only
fifteen minutes to present a rebuttal that summarized seventy
years of psychiatric and psychoanalytic opinion. When the
committee voted as planned, a few voices formally appealed to
the membership at large, which can overrule committee decisions
even on 'scientific' matters."

"The activists responded quickly and effectively. They drafted
a letter and sent it to over thirty thousand members of the APA
urging them to vote to retain the nomenclature change"

"Though the National Gay Task Force played a central role in
this effort, a decision was made not to indicate on the letter that it
was written, at least in part, by the Gay Task Force, nor to reveal
that its distribution was funded by contributions the Task force
raised". (R. Bayer, *Homosexuality and American Psychiatry: The
Politics of Diagnosis.*, Basic Books, 1981).

When the decision of 1973 was submitted to the membership of the American Psychiatric Association for ratification, only
58 percent voted to ratify it (Stein, 2000). In 1977 the journal

Medical Aspects of Human Sexuality reported on a survey showing that 69 percent of the psychiatrists disagreed with the decision because they consider homosexuality a disorder.

Two years later in 1975, when the American Psychological Association also removed homosexuality from its list of mental disorders, it too met with resistance. Today many of its members (currently over a thousand) belong to an organization known as the National Association for Research and Therapy of Homosexuality (NARTH), which regards homosexuality as a developmental disorder, though not a debilitating emotional disturbance.

A more recent survey, reported in 1993, indicates that disagreement continues among psychiatrists regarding the normalcy of homosexuality. A survey conducted by the American Psychiatric Association's Office of International Affairs showed that the majority of psychiatrist, world-wide, continue to view same-sex behavior as signaling pathology.

Contrasting Theories

This division of opinion on the issue of homosexuality is encouraged by two contrasting theories: *essentialist* and *constructivist*.

The *essentialist* theory views homosexuality as innate. It contends that individuals can be defined by their homoerotic desire and that these persons have shared fundamental characteristics throughout history and in different cultures.

The *constructivist* theory views homosexuality as constructed—as the product of larger social forces such as marketplace, urbanization, and government regulation. It believes that homosexual desire and gay and lesbian identity are variable and fluid in their origins and expression.

These theories also involve beliefs about the extent to which homosexuality is fixed or mutable. The *essentialist* position views sexual orientation as an essential characteristic of a person and therefore one that cannot be changed. On the other hand, the *constructivist* position implies that sexual orientation can be changed.

The apparent contradiction between these two theories, resembles those posed by earlier arguments as to what shapes a child—Is it nature or nurture? The coexistence of the two theories, *essentialist* and *constructivist*, explains why psychiatrists and psychologists are divided in their opinions regarding the complex phenomenon of homosexuality (Stein, 2000).

Differing Values

There is also professional division based on differing value orientations within mental health organizations such as the American Psychological Association. Though these organizations pose as being neutral, they are not. They have their own moral and value presuppositions. They teach what they believe is "good" (healthy, whole, adaptive, realistic, rational, mature.) They also identify what is "bad" (abnormal, pathological, immature, stunted, self-deceived). These clinical terms describe what the mental health professions view as good or bad behavior. In making these judgments they are, in fact, dealing with moral or value issues (Stanton Jones, 1994)

Take for instance the founder of rational-emotive therapy, Albert Ellis, and B.F. Skinner, founder of behaviorism. Both have based their scientific psychotherapies on the belief system of naturalism. Naturalism, like theism, is a faith-based, unprovable assumption—one that assumes that neither God nor the transcendent exist and that the material world is all there is.

If disbelief in the supernatural is acceptable among the control beliefs of some scientists, then belief in God and related beliefs about human persons should be allowable as control beliefs. Both theoretical orientations—neither of which can be proved—are legitimate as scientists acknowledge their position. Both are theories, and science needs theories, beliefs, hypotheses. Theories are necessary if one is going to understand or make sense of one's data. What is inaccurate is pretending that one's position is value neutral (Stanton Jones, 1994).

The current division of opinion among social scientists involves not only the issue of homosexuality but also a deeper issue that many psychologists find disturbing. It is the movement within these professions to adopt and promote social-political agendas such as radical feminism, sexual liberationism, and gay activism. To illustrate, the 1999 American Psychological Association Convention in Boston had 29 presentations on gay, lesbian, bisexual and transgender issues. Each was in favor of increasing rights for gays and discouraging efforts to change an individual's sexual orientation (Scharmann, 1999).

Values become evident in what an organization chooses to publish or to withhold from publication. A lead article in the *American Psychologist* (the one journal delivered to every member of the American Psychological Association), entitled "Deconstructing the Essential Father," concludes that fathers in two-parent heterosexual families are not necessary to the psychological health of children, that divorce does not irretrievably harm the majority of children, and that any harmful effects of divorce are related to economics rather than the absence of a father. The article seeks to promote a new view of the normative family.

Another indication of how this profession is leaning can be seen in the article published in the *Psychological Bulletin* (1998, vol. 124, p.22-53) related to pedophilia. The article identifies pedophilia as something that is not necessarily harmful to children when they willingly go along with the encounter. It refers to sexual abuse as a "value neutral term," suggesting that adult-adolescent sex may fall within the normal range. This article evoked strong protest from many psychologists and from Congress.

One can argue that these are simply isolated articles that may not represent a value orientation. But it should be noted that at a time when these articles were being published, presumably in the interests of airing all points of view, NARTH found it impossible to have accepted in an American Psychological Association (APA) publication an article showing that change of sexual orientation can be successful. The APA seemingly has closed its doors on information that contradicts its position. It is this politicization of APA, an organization that makes Ph.D. a requirement of membership and prides itself in seeking truth through objective research, that many psychologists find disturbing.

Two scientists from New Zealand, Neil and Briar Whitehead, were amazed at the extent to which the APA and related groups are politicized in their attitudes towards homosexuality. One of them wrote: "In my decades of experience as a research scientist and biochemist, I have seen no parallel in any other professional societies. This politicization of the facts may represent the most extreme example ever, outside of communist societies. I suggest the APA should be declared of unsound mind" (Whitehead, 1999).

Psychologist Robert Perloff, 1985 President of the American Psychological Association used even stronger words in a speech given to psychologists at their APA Annual Convention in 2001 In an expression of open anger and frustration he condemned the APA's one-sided political activism with respect to their policy on reorientation therapy of homosexuals.

He said: "You consider such therapy unethical....*That's all wrong*. First, the data are not fully in yet. Second, if the client wants a change, listen to the client. Third, you're barring research .How can you do research on change if therapists involved in this work are threatened with being branded as unethical?" (Monitor, Dec.01)

In a private correspondence with NARTH, Perloff who is a recipient of the American Psychological Foundation's Gold Medal Award for Lifetime Achievement in Psychology in the Public Interest, had this to say:

"I believe that APA is flat out wrong, undemocratic, and shamefully unprofessional in denying NARTH the opportunity to express its views and programs in the APA monitor and otherwise under APA purview."(Narth,Feb.2002)

Stifling Dissent

In a tolerant society it is essential that one tolerates views different from one's own. But in academia, where tolerance should be championed, dissent from the gay agenda is often not tolerated. It is dismissed with the accusation that the dissent is fomenting discrimination.

In the January 1998 issue of *Counseling and Values,* a journal of the American Counseling Association (ACA), an article was published entitled, "Counselor Bias in Working with Gay Men and Lesbians." In this article Steven Donaldson, a counselor who worked with homosexuals seeking to change their orientation, was critical of the discrimination directed at religious clients. He contended that believing homosexuality is desirable is not a "scientific" point of view but rather a philosophy akin to a bias. The question that a therapist faces, he suggested, is not, "Do I have a bias?" but "To which bias do I ascribe?" Therapists should be aware of their biases and be capable of discussing both sides of the issue with the client.

When NARTH asked for permission to reprint the article, it was turned down with this explanation:

The philosophy of your organization encourages those who want to "change" their sexuality to suppress their true identities and sends a very unfortunate message toward those who are content with their orientation. Your practice sanctions political and societal prejudice. Therefore, counselors attempting to practice the reorientation of gay men and lesbians are not in compliance with the professional standards for counselors.

The writer also indicated that the editor who had originally accepted Donaldson's article was no longer employed by the organization (Donaldson, 1998).

Professor Lynn Wardle, secretary-general of the International Society of Family Law, has experienced efforts to stifle dissent in his field. He finds that where there is overwhelming support for same-sex marriages and same-sex family styles there is little tolerance for those who disagree. Because of this he has written to encourage advocates of traditional marriage to speak up on behalf of the silent majority. He writes:

It is absolutely imperative that all of you accept as your personal responsibility, the duty of writing and raising your voice. You must not let these issues pass by uncontested. If you do, by your silence you have assented to these positions (Wardle, 2000).

An illustration of the kind of opposition he encounters occurred at a meeting of the family law section of the American Association of Law Schools, an annual conference that draws about 3000 law teachers each year. He was asked to participate in a panel discussion that considered from different points of view developments in the redefinition of the family. His task was to present the point of view that same-sex marriage and resulting family relations are not a good thing. This he did and in doing so raised concerns about the effects of same-sex parenting on children. He writes:

One lesbian law professor got up during the question period and began literally screaming at me. I can assure you that it had a very chilling effect upon the audience. After her embarrassing outburst, there was no one willing to express a point of view critical of gay or lesbian marriage or child-rearing. lest they be subject to the same kind of outburst.

Following a similar event, a friend came to him and said,"Lynn, I agree with what you had to say. Completely!" Wardle writes: "But he was unwilling to say that openly in the meeting for fear of the intimidation effect—particularly the outrage and hostile treatment that I had experienced" (Wardle, 2000).

The Inadequacies of an Inexact Science

Another source of disagreement among social scientists and mental health professionals has to do with research itself. Research does not produce ultimate truth. At best the findings of the social sciences represent an approximation of reality—an extension of one's senses. This is also true in the physical sciences where the principle of indeterminacy and chaos theory have shown that absolutes are usually not possible.

Because the social sciences represent a far less precise science, their findings can never be regarded as anything more than approximations of reality. As a result this discipline must be viewed as an ever-evolving science whose findings are always open to challenge, interpretation, and testing.

Because social science data are imprecise, one needs to know how the studies were carried out. Though one can always fault some aspect of a study, greater credence can be given to some studies than to others, based on their sampling, the method of collecting data, and the type of analysis.

Most importantly, if one is able to assemble many studies on a given subject—even though they are admittedly imprecise—and discover that they all point to the same conclusion, one can accept the findings as being based on fairly solid evidence. For this reason whoever uses research information must favor the findings of many studies (unless they all draw on one common flawed research base). This means that on any given subject a person who claims that his conclusions are based on the results of research needs to identify many studies and not a few.

Consider what this means. In the American Psychological Association there are 55 divisions, each focused on a different aspect of human functioning and inquiry. No psychologist can know the range of research in all 55 fields, not even in his or her own division. No one can know the thousands of published studies and be knowledgeable on all psychological topics.

Let me illustrate. I am a life member of the American Psychological Association and a Fellow in Division 36, "The Psychology of Religion." I served as editor of a book funded by Lilly Endowment, *Research on Religious Development: A Comprehensive Handbook* (1971). Its purpose was to consolidate all known research in this field and publish reviews on religious development. To accomplish this task 50 national scholars were involved. They reviewed thousands of studies in order to develop their reviews. Though only two percent of all published studies in the social sciences included the religious variable, we still located thousands of studies on the subject that were summarized in the handbook. This effort, which was considerable, did not go beyond the single subject area identified by Division 36.

Today we hear people insist that the position they espouse on homosexuality is based on "scientific studies." When I read their bibliography, I often discover that they are basing their position on disqualified studies or an inadequate sampling of the literature.

A striking illustration of this is found in a recent anthology, *Homosexuality and Christian Faith* (1999). It includes a chapter by a psychologist whose bibliography and statements reveal him to be woefully uninformed on this topic. For instance, he endorses the statement "there is no evidence" that efforts to help people change their sexual orientation is effective. What apparently he does not know is that more than 83 published studies have concluded that a homosexual orientation can be changed (Throckmorton, 1998).

Summary

All this points to the need for more open-ended research on homosexuality. As we have observed, psychologists and psychiatrists are seriously divided on the question, "Should homosexual behavior be considered normal?" Attempts have been made on both sides of the question to stifle discussion.

For the sake of homosexuals, especially those dissatisfied with their orientation and wishing to change, and for the sake of young people, this debate should not be cut off or limited. Rather, funding is needed for new research to expand our knowledge of this complex and puzzling topic, and free discussion should be welcomed by all sides.

Chapter Four

IS HOMOSEXUALITY
A HEALTHY LIFESTYLE?

Advocates of homosexuality present their orientation as a perfectly healthy lifestyle to be affirmed and celebrated. But is it healthy?

For some it is. There are the celibate and those who live in a committed relationship, who abstain from chemical abuse, and practice good health habits. These are people who often are major contributors to society. Many are well educated, upwardly mobile, financially secure people. A good example is Peter Gomes, an acknowledged homosexual, who is the Plummer Professor of Christian Morals at Harvard College. This well-loved pastor to Harvard students can be seen as a picture of health in his photo that appears on the dust jacket of his publication *The Good Book*. Another example is the musical genius, Leonard Bernstein, a known bisexual. This famed conductor and composer who lived a most strenuous life, continued creatively active until his death by cardiac arrest at age 72. Among lesbians there is Martina Navratilova, the internationally known tennis star. This remarkable athlete, a nine-time Wimbleton champion, was able to compete against the world's best tennis players.

The Dangers of Promiscuity

But good health is not a part of the lifestyle of many homosexuals, particularly promiscuous gays who engage in high-risk sexual behavior in public places This group has gained public exposure recently through six one-hour cable television presentations entitled, *Queer As Folk,* which focuses on a circle of gay and lesbian friends and presents what a reviewer labeled a stereotype of gays.

The premiere showing was welcomed by parties where gays gathered to celebrate what was seen as a breakthrough series and an historic event. At the start of the TV drama the narrator warns the audience with these words, "What you need to know is, it's all about sex." According to the reviewer of the series, the first hour presents the characters engaging in "orgies, stripteasing for business clients, male prostitution, shower-room sex, steam-room sex, equipment-room sex, Internet sex, club sex, and kitchen sex" (Justin, 2000).

This presentation surely is an embarrassment for gays who live a celibate or sexually responsible life, but it does represent the people who frankly acknowledge that promiscuity is a part of their lifestyle. In recent years it has been "politically incorrect" in some circles to raise questions about homosexual promiscuity and its health implications.

Professor Hadley Arkes, in his book *Making Sense of Homosexuality,* notes that "people who have serious doubts about the homosexual life must keep their opinions to themselves, because they are considered liabilities in corporations, law firms, and universities; there is a realistic fear, on the part of their employers, that the company could be the subject of an expensive anti-discrimination lawsuit" (Arkes, 1998). Perhaps as a result of this TV series, we may be able to have more open discussions on this topic.

As indicated in an earlier classification, there are gays for whom promiscuity is not a characteristic. They include devout members of religious groups as well as non-church gays who live quietly with a partner. The issue of promiscuity is however, a characteristic of those who champion gay sex in public places and those who are a part of the "leather" culture. Statements regarding the promiscuity of gays need to be largely associated with these two classifications. But how extensive is promiscuity for them? Is it more than characterizes certain subcultures of heterosexuals? Many insist there is no difference but lack data to substantiate their claim.

It is very difficult to compare gays with heterosexuals on the issue of sexual promiscuity because there is no master list of gays from which a random sample can be selected for survey purposes. The only valid comparison was made by staff of the National Opinion Research Center of the University of Chicago. Using a national random sample of 3,432 persons, a methodologically sound survey (1994), they were able to isolate the two samples for comparison.purposes.

The comparison had to do with the number of lifetime sexual partners reported by gays and the number reported by heterosexual men. Though gays reported a higher average in numbers (e;g; 260% higher than heterosexuals) the sample of gays (n = 30) was too small to show a statistically significant difference when submitted to a test of significance.

Some gays, however, are very willing to describe their culture as one where promiscuity is an important part of being gay. One such person is Frank Browning, a gay journalist for National Public Radio, who has described what he witnessed during the years 1989-1994. His description is amply summarized by the title of his book:: *The Culture of Desire:Paradox and Perversity in Gay Lives Today.* In this book he provides a candid account of what life is like in the gay districts of New York, San Francisco, Houston, Chicago, and Los Angeles. In his judgment a characteristic of these gay wards is namely,"sex for its own sake—raw, naked, wanton sex" (p.79).

A spokesperson for this culture, Bersoni,, whom Browning chooses to quote, criticizes gays outside their culture, who seek to desex gay life and recast gay people as just another community of polite American consumers for whom sexual acts are merely incidental private behavior.(p.80) He believes that gay men's obsession with sex should be celebrated rather than being denied. (p.91).

Browning ,who chooses to speak on behalf of his culture, is very frank about what he has seen and enjoys. He writes:" Any residual doubt about the place of sex—hot, sweaty, raunchy sex— in the AIDS prevention campaign, disappeared at the fifth global conference on AIDS in Montreal. For five days the discos were packed with gay doctors, nurses, activists, and researchers shamelessly cruising one another. A nearby bath house was doing land-office business" (p.119).

He adds, "Most of my straight friends have told me that they cannot fathom how an AIDS conference can also be a sex carnival. My standard, flip response has frequently been, 'But what else could it be? The lust of men for other men has not evaporated just because funerals and memorial services have become nearly as ordinary as an evening at the theatre.(p.120).

Browning, thoughtfully finishes his chapter entitled, "Spirit and Transgression", with these words: "Nowhere can sex be altogether safe, because sex is, for most of us, our primary, residual, atavistic connection to the realm of animal existence" (Browning, 1994,p.105).

The culture he describes is encouraged by a variety of publications aimed at gay intellectuals, gay travelers, gay Latinos, gay African Americans, S&M aficionados, leather aficionados, transsexuals, latex fetishists, Faerie mystics, high-tech nerds, nature lovers, wolf cubs looking for daddy bears, and white boys in suits.(p.192). It is a culture foreign to people of the church.

Promiscuity, a reality for many gays, is a phenomenon well documented by several major studies.

A.Bell and M.Weinberg (1978) in a study entitled, *Homosexualities: A Study of Diversity Among Men and Women,* showed that 28 percent of homosexual males had sexual encounters with 1000 or more partners. Furthermore, 79 percent said that more than half of their sex partners were strangers. In that survey only one percent of sexually active men had fewer than five life partners. This study is not based on a random sample but rather on gays involved in the sexually permissive sub-culture of San Francisco.

M.Pollack on the basis of his study (1985) reports that homosexual relationships seldom last more than two years. He describes sexual behavior among gays as "an average of several dozen partners a year" and "some hundreds in a lifetime" with "tremendous promiscuity." Again, this study is not based on a representative sample but represents a distinct subculture.

One of Germany's leading sexologists, Martin Dannecker (1991), himself a gay man, completed a study of 900 male homosexuals living in a "steady relationship." Of these men, 83 percent said they had frequent homosexual contacts outside of their primary relationship during a 12-month period. The average number per person was 115.

One of the most careful studies of stable homosexual pairs was researched and written by two authors who are themselves a homosexual couple—a psychiatrist and a psychologist. These two men, D. McWhirter and A. Mattison, published the findings of their study of 156 male couples, two-thirds of whom had entered into a relationship with the expectation of sexual fidelity. In their book, *The Male Couple: How Relationships Develop* (1984), the authors acknowledge that only seven of the couples had been able to maintain sexual fidelity. Furthermore of these seven, none had been together more than five years. The non-random sample used in this study is of gays living in San Diego during the 70's.

The *Comprehensive Textbook for Psychiatry* points out the health issue that is created by this promiscuity. "In general, gay men have increased rates of sexually transmitted diseases, HIV infection, and use of certain substances such as inhaled nitrites (poppers)." It continues:

> Since the 1980s the influence of HIV infection and AIDS on the individual lives and the communities of gay men has been enormous and has affected almost every aspect of the personal and public experience of being gay. As a result, HIV infection must be considered as a potential problem in the life of every gay man who enters the health care system, in relation to such issues as testing for HIV infection, ensuring early treatment intervention in infected individuals, preventing further HIV infection, responding to fears about contracting the disease, dealing with the chronic stress resulting from pervasive loss and illness, and taking care of gay men who are already infected (Sadock and Sadock, 2000).

A report from the Center for Disease Control and Prevention shows that for all years from 1985 to 1997, the chief contributor to acquired immunodeficiency syndrome (AIDS) in the United States has been men having sex with men. The average incidence for all ten years that is credited to homosexual behavior is 49.5 percent. Injecting drug use is involved in half that many, namely, 24.7 percent of the cases. Heterosexual contact accounts for no more than 9.1 percent. Clearly homosexual behavior has contributed to the spread of this dread disease in the United States (National Center for Health Statistics, 1999).

In Africa, however, that situation is reversed. There heterosexual activity is the chief contributor to the spread of this dread disease. And this is true in other countries as well. According to a United Nations report in the year 2000, the number of people infected world wide with HIV/AIDS was 36.1 million. In 12 months the number had increased by 5.3 million. In the words of former U.S. Secretary of State, Madeline Albright, the world is losing its fight with this disease. As a result of this report some pessimistic voices are claiming that soon everyone will be touched by HIV or AIDS.

In addition to the scourge of HIV, which brings with it fear and a tragic outcome, homosexual men are especially vulnerable to a host of other serious and sometimes fatal infections. These are caused by the entry of feces into the bloodstream. These include rare conditions known as the "Gay Bowel Syndrome," a condition that applies equally well to heterosexuals who use this method of intercourse.

A major review article summarizes the health threat in this way. Those involved in anal intercourse "are at particularly high risk of acquiring hepatitis B, giardiasis. amebiasis, shigellosis, campylobacteriosis, and anorectal infections with Neisseria gonorrhoea, Chlamydia trachomatous, Treponema pallidum, herpes simplex virus, and human papilloma viruses" (Judson, 1984).

The health threatening aspect of the homosexual lifestyle, however, is often muted by gays. An example is found in the focus of the 1989 Fifth International Conference on AIDS in Montreal. The meeting opened with a presentation of the AIDS manifesto demanding "full legal recognition of lesbian and gay relationships." Elizabeth Whelan, president of the American Council on Science and Health who was present and reported to the *New York Times*, concluded that the aim of the conference was not to save lives but to advance a political agenda (Whelan, 1989).

A contributing factor to their ill health is homosexuality's association with alcoholism and drug use. According to the National Gay-Lesbian Health Foundation, drug and alcohol problems are three times greater among gays than among heterosexuals (Insight, 1990).

This is confirmed in the current issue (2000) of Kaplan and Sadock's *Comprehensive Textbook of Psychiatry*. While acknowledging the difficulties in securing controlled studies which compare groups of heterosexuals with gays and lesbians, it states: "Alcohol and other substance abuse appear to be increased among gay men and lesbians with an incidence perhaps as much as two to three times higher than in the general population."

It adds, "Substances are often used to disinhibit prohibitions on sexual expression, and as a result many lesbians and gay men develop their sexual behaviors and patterns in relation to their use of these substances" (Sadock and Sadock, 2000).

Another health hazard noted particularly among gay, lesbian, or bisexual youth is the increased risk for attempting suicide.

Distress over homosexual thoughts, the invisibility of sexual-minority young people, and the lack of adequate resources to address their health and mental health needs increases for these youth the likelihood of suicide.

Two studies reported in the October 1999 issue of *Archives of General Psychiatry* find significantly higher levels of pathology in the gay population than the heterosexual population. One researcher, Michael Bailey in "Commentary: Homosexuality and Mental Illness" wrote:

> These studies contain arguably the best published data on the association between homosexuality and psychopathology, and both converge on the same unhappy conclusion: homosexual people are at substantially higher risk for some forms of emotional problems, including suicidality, major depression, and anxiety disorder.

> Subjects whom they classify as gay, lesbian, or bisexual were at an increased lifetime risk for suicidal ideation and behavior, major depression, generalized anxiety disorder, conduct disorder, and nicotine dependence at odds ratios of 2.8 to 6.2 when compared with the heterosexual sample.

Dr. Michael Bailey predicted that these findings would be interpreted in different ways.

1. By sexual-orientation therapists, as vindication that homosexuality should not have been removed from the diagnostic manual in 1973 because of its association with psychopathology.

2. By social conservatives as evidence of the consequences of promiscuity and an unhealthy lifestyle.

3. By gay activists as proof of the stresses of society's homophobia.

He cautioned that commitment to any of these three positions would be premature (Bailey, 1999).

Are Some Heterosexuals as Promiscuous?

Some respond to the topic of gay promiscuity with the argument that heterosexuals are as promiscuous as homosexuals. They base their evidence on accounts they read in the media about today's sex culture, the basketball players who boast about their thousands of sexual conquests, the growing number of young adults who are involved in premarital intercourse, and the "johns" who make prostitution a profitable business.

To answer this question a study is needed that focuses on certain subgroups such as the young adult unmarrieds, entertainment celebrities, the much divorced crowd involved in serial marriages, the many who use web sites for computer sex, the young adult sex clubs, or the professional athletes who are constantly surrounded by admiring groupies. These subgroups may constitute a more adequate comparison with homosexuals, who are in reality a subgroup in our society.

If we move beyond anecdotes to reliable studies, we can find a partial answer to the question in the book, *Sex in America*. Based on the only comprehensive and methodologically sound survey of America's sexual practices and beliefs, it is a study carried out by the staff at the National Opinion Research Center of the University of Chicago. They gathered their information through an hour-and-a-half interview of 3,432 respondents randomly selected nationally. Note the following quotations from the report of Michael, Gagnon. Laumann, and Kolata(1994).

> Despite the popular myth that there is a great deal of adultery in marriage, our data and other reliable studies do not find it. Instead a vast majority are faithful while the marriage is intact (p.89).

> We find that nearly all Americans have a very modest number of partners, whether we ask them to enumerate their partners over their adult lifetime or in the past year. Once married, people tend to have one and only one partner, and those who are unmarried and living together are almost as likely to be faithful (p.101).

> These findings give no support to the idea of a promiscuous society or of a dramatic revolution reflected in huge numbers of people with multiple, casual sex partners. Once married, the vast majority have no other sexual partner (p.105).

What about the young, unmarried population? We do have some reliable evidence regarding the incidence of premarital intercourse among high school students. It comes from a sample of 254,634 students gained by Search Institute from 460 public school districts located in 32 states. Though not a random sample its findings show percentages that are slightly higher than those found in other major studies.

The percentage of sophomores found to be sexually active is 19 percent and for seniors it is 26 percent. We know that when the sexual activity of American youth is compared with those in other technically advanced countries, the United States has the dubious distinction of being a leader in teenage pregnancy (Benson, 1977).

Summary

Is the homosexual lifestyle healthy? Again, we have no easy answer because there is no one homosexual lifestyle.

Some gay individuals or couples lead exemplary lives, avoiding risky behaviors, following good habits of nutrition and health care. On the other hand, it is important to say clearly that there is a strong tendency within the homosexual community toward promiscuity and very high-risk behavior, with the resultant risks for AIDS and other sexually transmitted diseases. There are also for homosexuals increased risks for alcoholism, drug abuse, and suicide.

Such risks cause us to question whether homosexuality should be endorsed without question. Out of concern for homosexuals and their families, and for the sake of young people, such threats should not be covered up but openly discussed. At the same time, support should also be given those homosexuals who are choosing to live a healthy, responsible lifestyle.

Chapter Five

CAN A HOMOSEXUAL ORIENTATION BE CHANGED?

As with other aspects of homosexuality, there is wide and sharp disagreement in the general public and among psychotherapists about whether a homosexual orientation can be changed.

Many homosexuals have tried valiantly to be heterosexual. Some have married and even fathered children in the hopes of being "normal." They have tried through self-help, psychotherapy, and prayer to change their orientation, and the change has not taken place. Some of these people are members of our Christian churches —living either in secret or as celibates or in committed relationships.

On the other hand, as we see in this chapter, reliable research evidence shows that a significant number of homosexuals have changed their orientation, totally or in part, through various forms of psychotherapy or through faith-based programs.

And then there is the militant gay agenda, supported by some—but not all—psychologists and psychiatrists, that claim sexual orientation is not possible and should not be attempted.

That is the position of the American Psychological Association made evident in "Guidelines for Psychotherapy With Lesbian, Gay, and Bisexual Clients," published in the December 2000 issue of the *American Psychologist*. The 16 guidelines developed by the Division 44/Committee on Lesbian, Gay, and Bisexual Clients indicate that a psychologist either harbors prejudice or is misinformed who would agree with a client "the only effective strategy for coping with conflict or discrimination is to seek to change the person's sexual orientation." Referring to the APA Ethics Code, Guideline 4 indicates that "these sections include prohibitions against discriminatory practices (e.g., basing treatment on pathology-based views of homosexuality or bisexuality), a prohibition against the misrepresentation of scientific or clinical data," (for example, the unsubstantiated claim that sexual orientation can be changed) (*American Psychologist,* 2000).

Gay activists are adamant in claiming that homosexuality is not reversible. The possibility of change contradicts one of their basic premises, namely that one is born a homosexual. Allowing therapists to help people change their orientation contradicts the idea that homosexuality is a healthy, normal orientation.

Many oppose the idea of so-called *reparative* therapy which tries to help homosexuals change their orientation, because it gives the impression that homosexuality is undesirable. They insist that the very suggestion that homosexuals might want to change only contributes to discrimination and gay bashing. Therefore they resist any effort to provide treatment for homo-sexuals who wish to change. They insist that change is not pos-sible and that ex-gays remain so for only a short time.

According to Jones and Yarhouse the most influential opposition to change programs comes from Douglas Haldeman, past president of the Division for the Psychological Study of Lesbian, Gay, and Bisexual Issues in the American Psychological Association. His critique which is unfailingly negative, accuses the various studies to which he makes reference as being "founded on heterosexual bias" and "homophobia". He speaks of change from heterosexuality into homosexuality as a revelation of ones true sexual identity but views any change from homosexuality back to heterosexuality as only superficial and ingenuous

Authors Jones and Yarhouse conclude that "his method is basically this: he examines past research and concludes, based on his prior commitment to the belief homosexuality cannot be changed, that any evidence of change must necessarily have occurred in non-homosexual (that is ,bisexual) patients. He implies that naïve and homophobic researchers must have made bad categorizations of their research, mixing homosexuals, bisexuals, and others."

"Haldeman would have us rush to the judgment that treatment has been a failure when any vestige of homosexual attraction remains .We would not declare alcoholism treatment to be a failure on the basis of some continuing attraction to alcohol or even occasional relapses to alcohol consumption" (Jones & Yarhouse, 2000, p.143).

Opposition to Re-orientation Therapy

The strong opposition to reparative or re-orientation therapy is seen in the efforts of gay activists to prevent ex-gays from telling their story. This occurred at the fifth annual "Coming Out of Homosexuality Day" conference in San Francisco's Park Auditorium. Assault and battery charges were made against two assailants who hit ex-gay speaker Michael Johnston with pies and hissed and booed ex-lesbian speaker Yvette Cantu.

A similar effort was made to prevent reparative therapists from gathering in convention. A group tried to disrupt the 1998 convention of NARTH (National Association for Research and Therapy of Homosexuality) October 1998, in Los Angeles. First, they succeeded in convincing the Beverly Hilton to cancel NARTH's reservations for the meeting room though a $5000 down payment had been made—and later refunded. When the conference was moved to another hotel, gay protestors stormed the door of the conference until they were removed by police. Outside the hotel they continued to parade with placards such as the one which read "NARTH—National Association of Repression, Tyranny and Hatred" (NARTH Bulletin, 1998).

Opponents of reparative or re-orientation therapy claim that it is "dangerous" and ineffectual in bringing about lasting change.

The accusation of this therapy being "dangerous," however, can apply to any form of psychotherapy. Anecdotal accounts are always available of how various therapies have been conducted in unethical and unprofessional ways, but I have yet to see a study in the professional journals that identifies reparative therapy as having been harmful when conducted by a trained and sensitive professional. On the contrary, Throckmorton's review of all published reports on reparative therapy found in 83 scientific journals resulted in his conclusion that such therapy has been effective and can be conducted in an ethical manner (Throckmorton, 1998).

What is really harmful is the failure to provide help to persons who are dissatisfied with living as a homosexual. Many of these are living despondent and tragic lives. Alan Medinger, who had been a practicing homosexual for 17 years, describes his marriage as disastrous. He said, "My wife and I had two children and in the later years only the facade of a marriage. I was unable to function heterosexually in the marriage."

"When I first came out of homosexuality, the initial changes in me were extraordinary. My feelings towards my wife changed radically; my sexual compulsion was broken, and I started to understand what my role should be in my family. I knew that I was called to a role of leadership in the family. I tried to fill this role— and I fell flat on my face. I simply couldn't do some of the things a man was called to do. This was an extremely painful time in my life. I struggled and struggled but just couldn't do much better simply by trying harder. From the writings of Leanne Payne and others, I started to understand what being masculine is."

Interestingly, Medinger found that softball games played with other homosexuals was a healing experience. Why? "Because it was fear—primarily of humiliation—that caused us to bail out of the world of boys when we were youngsters."

Medinger, who has been out of homosexuality for more than 20 years, founded and served as director of Regeneration, one of the oldest and largest Christian groups that helps people overcome homosexuality. His experience illustrates that a change in sexual orientation takes time and requires the development of the masculine side of one's being (Medlinger, 1994).

As will be documented later in this book, many homosexuals have made lifelong changes in their sexual orientation. These changes present compelling evidence that there are exceptions to the theory that a homosexual orientation is an immutable genetic predisposition.

However, gay activists are quick to challenge this conclusion by referring to people who have changed their orientation for a while and then reverted back to homosexuality. They insist that this "revolving door" phenomenon characterizes those who have made the break and returned to a heterosexual life. For that reason they cannot accept stories of people who have changed their orientation.

The fact that some do revert to their former orientation should not surprise us. Such reversions happen in every type of psychotherapy. That is why persons treated for alcoholism will refer to themselves as an "alcoholic" even though they have been alcohol free for years. They realize that the possibility is always present for returning to their former condition.

Opposition from the American Psychiatric Association

A statement against trying to change homosexual orientation is found in a recent decision of the American Psychiatric Association Board of Trustees. At their December 1998 meeting they endorsed a position statement opposing therapeutic techniques that some psychiatrists and mental health professionals claim can shift an individual's sexual orientation from homosexual to heterosexual.

When endorsing this decision, APA president Rodrigo Munzo said, "There is no scientific evidence that reparative or conversion therapy is effective in changing a person's sexual orientation" (*Psychiatric News*, December 14, 1999).

The position he espoused, however, is not shared by all who are involved in the leadership of the American Psychological Association. The APA president in 1998, Martin Seligman, published a book entitled, *What You Can Change and What You Can't*. The research he cites is optimistic about change for those who have had few homosexual experiences or who have bisexual feelings. and is more pessimistic for those who have had more long-term, ingrained homosexual feelings and activities.

In a letter which I received from Patrick DeLeon, president of the American Psychological Association, he states categorically: "The APA's resolution does not take the position that psychotherapeutic treatment to alter sexual orientation is harmful."

An article published in 1998 in the APA *Psychotherapy* journal entitled, "When Clients Seek Treatment for Same-Sex Attractions: Ethical Issues in the Right to Choose," states:

> Psychologists have an ethical responsibility to allow individuals to pursue treatment aimed at curbing experiences of same-sex attraction or modifying same-sex behaviors, not only because it affirms the clients rights to dignity, autonomy, and agency, as persons presumed capable of freely choosing among treatment, modalities, and behavior, but also because it demonstrates regard for diversity (Yarhouse, 1998).

In contrast to this position, opposition to reorientation therapy has become a public issue. In November, 1999 the mental health organizations listed below authorized the sending of a booklet to all 14,700 U.S. superintendents of public school districts. It warned them that potential harm is posed by "reparative therapy" as well as by other techniques intended to change sexual orientation. The booklet states that "therapy directed specifically to changing sexual orientation is contraindicated, since it can provoke guilt and anxiety while having little or no potential for achieving changes in orientation."

The booklet makes specific reference to "transformational ministries" and other religiously based efforts that try to help homosexuals change their orientation. It gives a warning that endorsing or promoting such efforts could raise constitutional problems (Goode, 1999).

Cosponsors of the booklet include such mental health organizations as the following:

The American Psychiatric Association
National Association of Social Workers
American Academy of Pediatrics
American Psychological Association

The publication *Psychiatric News* (December 1999) informs us that this statement opposing reparative therapy was guided through the Assembly by Sved (only name given), the assembly's representative from the Caucus of Lesbian, Gay, and Bisexual Psychiatrists.

Response to the American Psychiatric Association

Here are quotes from a letter sent to the American Psychiatric Association and signed by five leading psychiatrists (names listed below) who know the research and have had a lifetime involvement in the therapy of homosexuals.

The homosexual patient, his family, and the worldwide psychiatric community should not be misled by what is actually sociopolitical activism within our organization, the aim of which is to normalize all homosexual behavior and to demean and discredit efforts by psychiatrists and psychoanalysts who attempt to help these patients and their families.

The conclusion by the board that reparative therapy has no efficacy in 'changing someone's sexual orientation' is not only false, but misleading and misguided. There are dozens of psychoanalytic reports that support the efficacy of treatment.

To cite simply one of them, as reported by H. MacIntosh, (1994), *Journal of the American Psychoanalytic Association* : "In response to a survey, 285 psychoanalysts (graduates of the Western Psychoanalytic Institute) reported having analyzed 1,215 homosexual patients. Their report shows that 23 percent changed to heterosexuality from homosexuality and 84 percent of the total group received significant therapeutic benefit."

The statement that psychoanalytic psychotherapy is "destructive" is completely false. Being homosexual against one's conscious will can become "destructive" when one is not given help, counseling, reassurance, and understanding.

Finally, the board's negative declarations regarding reparative therapy amount to a breach of our freedom to practice psychiatry (a freedom noted in Article One of our Constitution). This freedom to practice was unanimously protected in a Resolution passed by the American Psychoanalytic Association 5/20/93, which stated: "Scientific issues should be researched, discussed, and debated in a scientific atmosphere of free and open exploration. Threats to disrupt scientific meetings, intimidation of clinical researchers, and sexual politics have no place in our continuing attempts to understand human sexual behavior."

Those signing this letter to the APA include:

Charles W. Socarides, M.D., Clinical Professor of Psychiatry, Albert Einstein College of Medicine, 1979-1996; Life Fellow and Member American Psychiatric Association; Life Member, International Psychoanalytic Association; Fellow, American College of Psychoanalysts

Abraham Fredman, M.D., Fellow, American Psychiatric Association; Professor Emeritus Psychiatry, Thomas Jefferson College, Philadelphia

C. Downing Tait, M.D., Life Fellow, American Psychiatric Association; Former Professor of Psychiatry, Emory University

Bejamin Kaufman, M.D., Fellow, American Psychiatric Association; Clincal Professor of Psychiatry, University of California

Harold M. Voth, M.D., Life Fellow, American Psychiatric Association; Charter Fellow, American College of Psychoanalysts; Professor Emeritus of Psychiatry, University of Kansas

The Case for Re-orientation Therapy

Psychotherapists Joseph Nicolosi, A. Dean Byrd, and Richard Potts. write in their report "Towards the Ethical and Effective Treatment of Homosexuality" that disagreements between gay affirmative and conversion therapists about homosexuality and its treatment are rooted in conflicting assumptions and values about the nature of human beings, homosexuality, and the desirability and possibility of change.

Ultimately, a person's beliefs about whether or not homosexuality is desirable, normal, or moral is a value choice and cannot be resolved by scientific findings regarding etiology, prevalence, or treatment outcome. People of various cultures and religions have a right, therefore, to believe that homosexuality is not valuable and is best minimized and overcome, just as gay activists have the right to believe otherwise. (Nicolosi, Byrd & Potts,1998, page 6)

Reviews of the therapy-outcome literature published during this time period concluded that therapists had considerable success at helping homosexually-oriented people reduce or overcome their homosexual tendencies (Adams and Sturgis, 1977; Birk, 1974; Clippinger, 1974; Rogers, Roback, McKee and Callhoun, 1976). For example, Rogers et al. (1976) concluded: "Homosexuals can be successfully treated in group psychotherapy whether the treatment orientation is one of a change in sexual pattern of adjustment, or whether a reduction in concomitant problems is the primary goal."

The most compelling evidence is found in the paper by Warren Throckmorton, past president of the American Mental Health Counselors Association, published in1998 in *The Journal of Mental Health Counseling*. It gives a comprehensive review of published research in 83 scientific journals regarding the effectiveness and appropriateness of therapeutic efforts to change sexual orientation. Throckmorton reviews all the published articles on the outcomes of Psychoanalytic Approaches, Behavior Therapy Approaches, Cognitive Approaches, Group Psychotherapy Approaches, and Religiously Oriented Approaches. It is a very complete review of the scientific literature.

In summary he says:"Efforts to assist homosexually oriented individuals who wish to modify their patterns of sexual arousal have been effective. They can be conducted in an ethical manner, and should be available to those clients requesting such assistance" (Throckmorton, 1998).

This report by Throckmorton is strongly criticized by a number of authors because the studies he includes focus on varying aspects of homosexual behavioral change. That is true. Some of the studies focus on the extent of the patient's sexual behavior with other men, some on their increased sexual attraction to women, some on positive marital functioning, and some on decreased homosexual fantasy or attraction. All types of assessment, however, focus on one aspect, namely, homosexual change. Furthermore, the 83 studies represent the vast preponderance of the 101 found to have been reported on homosexual change between the years 1930-1976. Throckmorton's report provides reasonable evidence (not scientific proof) of homosexual reorientation that is ethical and effective for some.

Psychiatrist Robert Spitzer, a key player in the original 1973 decision to remove homosexuality from the *Diagnostic and Statistical Manual of Mental Disorders,* has become interested in studying the effectiveness of sexual reorientation therapies as a result of talking with former homosexuals. He was impressed by the ex-gays he met from Transformation Christian Ministries who staged a demonstration at the 1999 American Psychiatric Association convention demanding the right to sexual re-orientation therapy. They carried placards saying, "The APA Has Betrayed America with Politically Correct Science" and "APA—How Do You Explain 20,000 Former Homosexuals?"

Moved to rethink the issue of sexual-reorientation therapy, Spitzer said this during an interview with Dr. Laura Schlessinger, January 21, 2000. "I'm convinced from people I have interviewed, that for many of them, they have made substantial changes toward becoming heterosexual. . . . I came to this study skeptical. I now believe that for many, these changes can be sustained" (Nicolosi, 2000).

Spitzer's interest led him to arrange for a debate on reorientation therapy at the May 2000 annual convention of the American Psychiatric Association. The debate scheduled for Wednesday, May 17, was to feature two psychiatrists opposing this kind of therapy and two panelists speaking on behalf of reorientation.

The debate had to be canceled when the two psychiatrist scheduled to oppose the "therapy can be ethical and effective" position refused to participate. And no other psychiatrist was willing to debate against that position. One can assume they backed down because they were intimidated by the evidence and by the increasingly vocal group of ex-gays who have become disgusted with the American Psychiatrist Association's stranglehold on the discussion (Nicolosi, 2000).

The Success of Secular Psychotherapists

In his book *Homosexuality and the Politics of Truth* psychiatrist Jeffrey Satinover lists the therapeutic outcomes reported by nine psychotherapists who treated a total of 341 homosexuals. The average success rate for these psychiatrists was 52 percent (Satinover 1996).

J.A. Clippinger (1974), following his review of a number of psychoanalytic group and behavioral studies, concluded that for homosexuals seeking treatment "at least 40 percent of the homosexuals were cured and an additional 10-30 percent of the homosexuals were improved."

But what does "improved" mean? That expression seems strange because we tend to think of therapy as being either successful or unsuccessful in bringing about change. "Improved" means the person has come to see that he is on a different place on the continuum of sexual behavior. He has become less troubled by the thoughts and fantasies that drive him toward homosexual activity.

This concept of a continuum was made prominent by Alfred Kinsey, Director of the Institute for Sex Research at Indiana University. He devised a seven point scale (0-6) for evaluating the sexual behavior of men in which a 0 indicated a heterosexual, a 3 indicated a bisexual and a 6 indicated a homosexual (Money, 1998).

Kinsey's underlying assumption was that men's sexual behavior occupies different places on this scale of 0 to 6. Rather than viewing homosexuality and heterosexuality as discrete categories, he saw the possibility of both drives coexisting in a person with differing intensities. A person who entered therapy as a 6 and who was later classified as a 3 or 2 would be viewed as "improved" but not totally free from homosexual desires.

In the 1994 *Journal of the American Psychoanalytic Association,* a report surveyed 285 psychoanalysts who were graduates of the Western Psychoanalytic Institute. These therapists having psychoanalyzed 1,215 homosexual patients report that 23 percent changed to heterosexuality from homosexuality and 84 percent of the total group received significant therapeutic benefit. (MacIntosh, 1994). This report quoted in a letter to the American Psychiatric Association by five life members of the association, includes the comment that "the statement that psychoanalytic psychotherapy is 'destructive' is completely false."

E. C.James (1978) meta-analyzed 101 outcome studies published between 1930 and 1976. She concluded that when the results of all research studies were combined, approximately 35 percent of the homosexual clients "recovered" (returned to heterosexual orientation) and 27 percent "improved" (reduced their homosexual drive). Based on this finding she argued that pessimistic attitudes about the prognosis for homosexuals changing their sexual orientation are not warranted.

To inquire about a current success rate, I called psychotherapist Joseph Nicolosi, author of the book, *Reparative Therapy of Male Homosexuals*, who has counseled more than 1000 homosexuals. He said, "The success rate is the same as for any kind of psychotherapy: one-third success, one-third improved, and one-third unsuccessful."

A highly significant survey was carried out by psychotherapists Joseph Nicolosi, A. Dean Byrd, and Dr. Richard Potts of the University of Utah. In this study, *A Nationwide Survey of Dissatisfied Homosexually-Oriented People*, a sample was secured of 882 men (78%) and women (22%) who had been dissatisfied with their homosexual orientation and sought help. This sample was secured by using a "snowball" method in which each person who chooses to participate encourages others to take the survey. The 882 (men and women) who did choose to do so were people who through therapy or pastoral counseling had experienced change.

The purpose of the survey was to "explore the experiences of individuals who have struggled with homosexuality during a time in their lives, were dissatisfied with that orientation, and have since sought and experienced some degree of change."

Two thirds of those in this study (67.6%) perceived themselves as having been exclusively or almost entirely homosexual. After treatment or change, only one in eight (12.8%) perceived themselves in this manner. Before treatment or change only 2% of the respondents perceived themselves as exclusively or almost entirely heterosexual. After treatment or change, one third (34%) perceived themselves as that.

The average age for those entering conversion therapy was 30. The average length of time that had elapsed since experiencing a change in sexual orientation was 6.7 years. For 23 percent of the respondents, ten or more years had elapsed since experiencing their change of orientation.

A large majority (96%) of these 882 (men and women) respondents said that religious and spiritual beliefs played a crucial role in their healing and change from homosexuality. More than half (54%) had participated in reorientation therapy with a professional therapist .and 45% had received treatment from a non-professional therapist or pastoral counselor. A few made efforts to change on their own.

This study of 882 men and women identifies a "hidden" yet large group of dissatisfied homosexually-oriented men who have experienced conversion therapy, pastoral counseling, and/or self-help and benefitted from it. Not to be ignored are the positive changes in the feelings of well-being reported by these respondents. According to the psychological measures used in this study, the sample showed impressive gains in self-acceptance, self-understanding, trust of the opposite sex, self-esteem, spirituality, relationship with the church, relationship with God, overcoming depression, and gaining emotional stability. These changes could not be explained by chance factors (Nicolosi,Byrd,& Potts, 1998).

What does it mean to change? Joseph Nicolosi in *Reparative Therapy of Male Homosexuality* defines it as having "captured one's own nature." The assumption underlying his therapy is this: Every man, on some deeper level, is a heterosexual but struggling with a homosexual issue. The healing task is to demystify men and masculinity, it is to help the client experience himself as "one of the guys" and to receive the masculine affirmation that only a man can bestow upon another man. This affirmation, not sex, is the deepest need of the homosexual.

The key factor for change, however, is motivation. Without deep-seated commitment to personal change, the process of transitioning is virtually impossible (Cohen, 1994).

The Success of Religiously Oriented Approaches

A provocative article –one that required two years for peer review –was published in an official journal of the American Psychological Association in June of 2002. The article is unique in that it presents 11 studies of "ex-gays" which are focused on a religious faith as contributing to the process of changing from homosexual attractions to heterosexual ones.

The article by Warren Throckmorton begins early with a quote from F. Worthen whose article is found on the internet under the title, "Ex-gay: Fact, fraud, or fantasy? Worthen writes: "What does "ex-gay" mean? It is a statement of fact. I am no longer the same. God has changed me, He is changing me, and He most certainly will continue to change me".

He continues: "At New Hope Ministry, we do not attempt to make heterosexuals out of homosexuals. Rather, we attempt to change a person's identity, the way a person looks at himself. We encourage the former gay to drop the label homosexual from his life. However, we do not ask him to become dishonest about his struggle with homosexuality . He is a Christian who has a homosexual problem, rather than a homosexual who believes in Jesus Christ."(Worthen, 2000).

It is significant that in the study by Nicolosi, Byrd and Potts involving 882 individuals who tried sexual reorientation, 96% of the total sample said that religion was very important to them. It helped motivate them to seek change in their behavior.

In the study reported earlier by Robert Spitzer, religion also emerges as a contributing factor in the person's change. He notes that of the 200 he interviewed, 93% said that religion is "extremely" or "very Important" to them . Most of his subjects were Protestant Christians (81%). Their two most common reasons for seeking change were that living as a gay individual was no longer satisfying (81%) and that same-sex behavior was at odds with their religion (79%). (Spitzer, manuscript under review).

Many religiously-oriented organizations are involved in affecting sexual reorientation. In evaluating them Satinover (1996) notes that Exodus International, an umbrella organization for more than 100 separate ministries, represents a wide spectrum of openly religious approaches to the healing of homosexuality. However, many of these groups reflect an authoritarian approach and reject the contribution of psychology or psychotherapy.

One of the most successful of the religiously-oriented organizations is Desert Stream, headquartered in Los Angeles and led by Andrew Comiskey, a former homosexual. He reports that 50 percent of those who start his program complete it with substantial progress out of homosexuality into heterosexuality. Another ministry is called Redeemed Life founded by Mario Bergner who had been deeply involved in the east coast gay life. His therapeutic approach combines depth psychology with healing prayer.

Another healing ministry founded by Leanne Payne and centered in Wheaton, Illinois, is known as Pastoral Care Ministries. Her approach has been influenced by the "Healing of Memories" movement—associated with Anglicanism and Pentecostalism. In this approach the central activity for the healing of homosexuality is healing prayer.

W. E. Consiglio, founder of HOPE Ministries on the east coast, who has served for 15 years as a Christian therapist with homosexual people views homosexuality as being a disorientation or deviancy from a "God-given" heterosexual development. Hence the task he seeks to accomplish is a reorientation.

Ten years ago pastor Wendell Anderson and his wife Nancy established a counseling ministry known as Eagles Wings, an outgrowth of the ministry of North Heights Lutheran Church near St. Paul, Minnesota. Their approach is based on the belief that homosexual feelings are the result of unresolved emotional traumas, and unmet affirmation, love, and intimacy needs. They view homosexual behavior as a symptom of a reparative drive to meet these needs. They report success in freeing clients for a life of heterosexuality.

Religiously based support groups include the following:

Homosexuals Anonymous(HA)—Christian-based recovery network
Courage/Encourage—Catholic Ex-Gay Ministry / Parent's Ministry
JONAH—Jews Offering New Alternatives to Homosexuality
Evergreen International—Mormon Ex-Gay Ministry
One by One—Presbyterian Ex-Gay Ministry
Transforming Congregations—Methodist Ex-Gay Ministry

PFOX—Christian ministry for parents, spouses, family
members and friends.
Pastoral Care Ministries—Recovery through healing prayer.

The Much Quoted Claim—There is No Evidence

The claim "there is no scientific evidence that reparative therapy is effective" is being made by many responsible people. A most recent statement came from Surgeon General David Satcher in his report to the nation entitled *The Call to Action to Promote Sexual Health and Responsible Sexual Behavior.* In his report he categorically affirms : "There is no scientific evidence that sexual orientation can be changed" (page 7). The documentation he gives for his statement is Haldeman's article, "The Practice and Ethics of Sexual Orientation Conversion Therapy" (1994) and the policy statement of the American Psychiatric Association.

Because this claim is being presented to people in congregations it bears further scrutiny. We can begin by noting how studies are carried out by scientists.

Professor Stephen Hawking, the renown theoretical physicist, gives the following account of how scientific inquiry is conducted.

"A good theory will describe a large range of phenomenon on the basis of a few simple postulates and will make definite predictions that can be tested. If the predictions agree with the observations, the theory survives that test, though it can never be proved to be correct. On the other hand, if the observations disagree with the predictions, one has to discard or modify the theory. (At least that is what is supposed to happen. In practice, people often question the accuracy of the observations and the reliability and moral character of those making the observations.)" (Stephen Hawking, 2001).

Note that scientific inquiry proceeds by presenting a theoretical statement or hypothesis which then can be tested. Evidence is then summoned that will either support or reject the hypothesis. Note also, that evidence which supports the hypothesis does not prove that it is correct. It only strengthens the likelihood that what is proposed squares with reality.

Thus a scientist begins with an hypothesis such as —"Change from homosexual to heterosexual orientation is possible for some". That is a necessary first step. This hypothesis, or whatever hypothesis one uses, is tested by marshalling evidence to support or reject the hypothesis. The evidence which is used may vary a great deal and whatever it is, one can assume that it will be scrutinized carefully—as Hawking indicates from his experience. The evidence which a scientist might use to test the hypothesis posed above, might include survey findings, or the results of interviews, or data made available through carefully controlled experiments.

It is important to note that gay activist, Douglas Haldeman, in his article, "The Practice and Ethics of Sexual Orientation Conversion Therapy" debunks **all** research reporting successful reorientation. Having found some fault with the methodology of these studies, he proceeds to say there is no scientific evidence for sexual orientation conversion.

Should we use Haldeman's criteria for what is truly scientific, we could counter by saying: **There is no scientific evidence that reorientation conversions are not successful.** No longitudinal study has been carried out to demonstrate that this well established hypothesis is false.

It is important to note that most studies reporting a degree of success with conversion therapy appeared in professional journals during the 50's, 60's and 70's. Following the big "chill" in research that occurred after the decision of the American Psychiatric Association in 1973, the number of studies diminished rapidly (due to a lack of funding and the reluctance of editors to publish articles contesting the position of the American Psychiatric Association.

Unfortunately, the 83 studies reported by Throckmorton as evidence of conversion outcomes lack the sophisticated methodology that has come to characterize studies being carried out today. Furthermore, the studies use self-report which some claim is always invalid data because they believe information dealing with a threatened area of sexuality cannot be truthfully given. That, of course, remains an unproven assumption when applied to all self-report. It is an argument that could be used to fault almost all the reports which describe therapeutic outcomes for socially unacceptable and stigmatized behaviors such as drug use, alcoholism, parental neglect, theft, and spousal abuse.

The lack of sophisticated methodology, however, does not disprove the success of conversion treatments. One cannot dismiss conclusions of these studies on the basis of methodological limitations. One can only say the information is less reliable.

Reliability is an important concept because it establishes the ceiling for the validity of a study and its findings. The more reliable a study, the greater is the likelihood that its findings will be found to be valid. We are familiar with this idea of reliability having noted how attentive FBI agents are to the reliability of information on purported terrorist attacks. They examine for reliability and then decide on what should be believed.

This concept of reliability is especially important to outcome research (namely, what happens as a result of therapy). It is known that some outcome information is low in reliability and some ranks high.

Grading the strength of evidence is commonly done in the medical sciences where studies are evaluated and graded by a team of researchers (not one)—such as the Institute for Clinical Systems Improvement. Their people evaluate the strength of the evidence on the basis of design type, sample size, and patient population. The study is assigned one of four grades: Grade I—supported by good evidence; Grade II—supported by fair evidence; Grade III—supported by limited evidence; and Grade IV—supported only by opinion (Greer N, Mosser G, Logan G, Halaas G-2000).

Note my informal grading of information sources which are commonly used in psychiatric studies. I have ranked them beginning with those that yield the least reliable information to those providing the most reliable evidence.

1. **Anecdote** ("I know someone who.") This is the least reliable information because for every anecdote that is used another can be given that gives just the opposite information. Yet it is often used. Haldeman, for instance, used an anecdote to fault the reported result of change claimed by a religious therapist. An anecdote about a single individual provides no information about the distribution of possible anecdotes, pro and con.

2. **Therapist Report**. Conclusions here are based on progress the therapist observed in weekly meetings over a period of two or three years. These reports lack a follow-up (did they really change?). Also, unreliability centers in the fact the therapist may have misjudged a client or two. The reports of therapists are really case studies useful for developing hypotheses.

3. **Client's Report.** When 10 to 20 clients report how they have changed, one has a more reliable report and stronger evidence

because many, not one person's evaluation, is involved. But some clients, concerned over their stigmatized behavior or wanting to please the therapist, might misrepresent their report.

4. **Follow-up Studies**. Greater reliability can be accorded to self-reports given five years or more after therapy. For instance, considerable credence can be given to the evidence made available through Spitzer's study of 200 persons who had been ex-gays for five years or longer. He concludes from his interviews that most have indeed changed.

5. **Follow-up Using Questionaires.** Even greater reliability can be accorded the report from 882 ex-gays, a fourth of whom had experienced change for ten years or more. Their self-report is given anonymously by means of a questionnaire,where reticence due to stigmatized behavior is hardly an issue. I quote this study elsewhere in this book, giving some detail because it represents highly reliable information.

6. **Self-Report With an Objective Assessment.** Penile plethysmography invented by Freund has been a useful scientific instrument for assessing the reliability of a sexual offender's report. Several researchers have been using this objective measure. Though it is limited by false positives, it provides an objective method of assessing the extent to which erotic fantasies or same-sex arousal has diminished or remains with a patient. It promises to be valuable if and when a longitudinal study is made of ex-gays.

7. **Experimental and Control Groups.** In pharmaceutical studies an experimental drug is given to one group and a placebo to another. Once the experiment is over, the study is replicated to see if the findings hold. This is the most reliable kind of outcome study for testing a hypothesis. It is the kind of study we used at Search Institute to assess the outcomes that occurred when youth extended friendship to alienated youth (not homosexual youth).

Can the information from studies of varying degrees of reliability be used as evidence to support the hypothesis that change is possible for some? Yes, under certain conditions. If the preponderance of studies on a given subject all point to the same conclusion, one can legitimately hypothesize that these provide a degree of scientific support even if their research designs are not perfect. Studies do not prove that an hypothesis is correct. They simply provide added support for considering the hypothesis to be true.

Note how hypothesis testing proceeds. When Spitzer, chair of the committee that removed homosexuality from the category of mental illness, became interested in the reversibility of homosexuality he began interviewing persons who had been ex-gays for five years or more. He reported his findings at the May, 2001 convention of the American Psychiatric Association.

His first slide made it apparent that the hypothesis he had been holding was this—"Homosexual behavior... can never be changed." The slide read:
"There is a professional concensus that homosexual behavior can be resisted, renounced or relabeled but that homosexual orientation can never be changed."

His next slide read: "I certainly shared this viewpoint."

He then described how he had talked with some ex-gays who were picketing at the 1999 APA meeting claiming that, contrary to a recent APA position statement , change of sexual orientation was possible. After much thought he decided to study the self-reported experiences of individuals who claim to have achieved a change from homosexual to heterosexual attraction.

The evidence resulting from his interviews of 200 (143 males and 57 females) by telephone caused him to reject the hypothesis he had been holding. He indicated this in the slide that read:
"Contrary to conventional wisdom, some highly motivated individuals, using a variety of change efforts, can make substantial change in multiple indicators of sexual orientation and achieve good heterosexual functioning. Subjects that made less substantial changes still believed that such changes were extremely beneficial".

Here is what he reported as evidence. During the year prior to initiating change 99% of the male sample and 88% of the females affirmed that they had same-sex sexual fantasies while after they had experienced change, only 32% of the men and five percent of the women reported the same type of fantasies. A desire for emotional involvement with same-sex individuals went from 78% of the men and 81 % of the women to eight percent of men and four percent of women post-change (Spitzer, manuscript under review).

He ended his presentation with words he heard several of his subjects give spontaneously. "I have no problem accepting that most gays have no interest in changing. I wish they could also acknowledge that I have a right to change and that I have." Though one can identify methodological limitations in Spitzer's study, the evidence is compelling.

The same can be said for the questionnaire study by Nicolosi, Byrd and Potts involving 882 ex-gays. These are the ones who had sought help because they were dissatisfied with their orientation. The survey showed that approximately seven years after initiating change, 34% could report much change towards heterosexuality, and 43 % could report some change. This evidence supports the hypothesis that reorientation is possible for some.

Importantly, the purpose of scientific inquiry is to gain a greater understanding of reality. The objectivity which characterizes this pursuit allows for various hypotheses to be proposed and tested. Because the evidence resulting from one study is never conclusive, it needs to be replicated in a variety of ways. The evidence Spitzer found through his interviews, provides another indication that the hypothesis regarding homosexual change cannot be rejected as false. Other studies are needed to increase one's confidence in the truth of this hypothesis.

Summary

To summarize: There is strong opposition to the idea that a homosexual orientation can be changed, both from the gay community and from many psychotherapists who claim that reorientation or reparative therapy does not work and is even dangerous.

Yet, as we have seen, reliable studies show that lasting sexual reorientation is possible for some—but not all—homosexuals. For the sake of those who seek to change their orientation, information about both secular and religious therapies should be made available in our churches and communities. And those homosexuals who cannot change or do not want to change warrant our wlcome and support.

Chapter Six

A DILEMMA FOR THE CHRISTIAN CHURCH

There are countless Christians who are homosexuals but not by choice. Their sexual orientation is the result of factors most of which are outside their control.

When Project Director Carolyn Riehl reported on her interviews of 35 gays and lesbians serving as pastors in the Evangelical Lutheran Church in America, she said: "For almost all, coming to understand themselves as gay or lesbian was a gradual process, fraught with guilt, shame, confusion, danger, loneliness, and loss." As one said, "I knew in my heart of heart that I was homosexual, but I prayed that God would take these feelings from me" (Riehl,1998).

Mel White has become the spokesperson for this group of Christians found in every denomination. For 25 years he concealed these feelings from his wife while carrying out an effective ministry of teaching at Fuller Seminary, serving as pastor in a large Covenant church, producing prize winning films, writing bestseller books, and serving as ghostwriter for Jerry Falwell, Pat Robertson, Corizion Aquino, Oliver North, and the Southern Baptist leader D. T. Criswell.

While being involved in these highly visible ministries, he was fighting to rid himself of his inner desire for homosexual love. He took advantage of every solution being offered him but to no avail.

In his book *What's So Amazing About Grace* (1997), Philip Yancey, a friend of Mel White, tells about the night when Mel called him from a fifth-floor balcony over-looking the Pacific Ocean, declaring, "You have ten minutes to tell me why I should not jump." Phillip Yancey's pleadings, which used every argument he could summon, were successful.

Mel White finally told his wife about his homosexual orientation, and subsequently the two suffered through a heart-wrenching divorce. They separated in a loving way, continuing to co-parent their two children and provide for their needs. Evidence of his effort to live out his Christian faith as a gay Christian is seen in the loving preface that his wife wrote for his book, *Stranger at the Gate* (1994).

Mel White became co-chair of Soulforce, a militant organization dedicated to using civil disobedience to force denominations to accept homosexuals as God's creation. In a letter to the *Christian Century* he writes, "Our nonviolent demonstration at Cleveland is just the first step. These acts of 'media-driven street theater' signal the launch of a long-term Soulforce program of civil disobedience and noncooperation at other national and regional conferences, conventions, and assemblies. Call it what you will, but plan for it at your denominational headquarters, at your seminaries and colleges, and even at your individual churches across the country" (White, 2000).

The dilemma for the church centers not only in the fact that such Christians are part of the church, but also that these Christians are convinced their sexual orientation is God-given, a life to be celebrated and enjoyed. They insist that homosexuality is a gift of God, that this orientation is irreversible, and that homosexuality is as normal as heterosexuality. These gay Christians believe that the rights and privileges accorded heterosexuals should also be theirs, and this includes ordination of non-celibate gays and the blessing of same-sex-marriages.

These people are calling for the church to become a place both of reconciliation and justice. One group, Lutherans Concerned, prepared a carefully and thoughtfully written paper entitled, *A Call For Dialog*. It asks for open discussions on gay and lesbian issues for the purpose of breaking down the church's walls of denial and avoidance. Its stance is clear. There are only two positions: 1) a same-gender orientation is flawed, or, 2) a same gender orientation is God-given. A middle ground is rejected (Ballew, 1985).

Craig Staller, a homosexual, writes a moving account in the *Christian Century* of his struggle to give up his ordination rights in order to acknowledge publicly his relationship with Doug. As a "practicing" homosexual and now ex-clergy, he speaks of the pain that is his in being shut out from the work he loves and did well (Staller, 2001).

The Position of the Religious Right

Complicating the dilemma is the hate being engendered against gays and lesbians by some people on the religious right. In his fund-raising letter Jerry Falwell identifies the goal of gays and lesbians as being "the complete elimination of God and Christianity from American society [and this goal] is being designed right now." However, he recently (2000) modified his position and demonstrated this change by a public and much publicized meeting with Mel White.

In a letter to 5000 pastors in Oregon, where he was well known as pastor and seminary professor, White identified himself as a homosexual. He urged the pastors to oppose Measure Nine that would disenfranchise every gay and lesbian in the state. He received 80 letters in response, only two of them positive. One pastor called him "cursed of God"; another averred that he should be "put to death for his sinfulness" (White, 1994).

This climate of condemnation, generated by some on the religious right, complicates the situation for people who wish to view this issue from the perspective of Scripture and reliable research. The law orientation of such people stands in opposition to an approach that is ministry oriented.

At Search Institute we carried out a study of Lutherans that empirically established that there are two types of church members—those whose orientation is grace and those whose orientation is law. Those with a law orientation tend to be more concerned with an absolute following of rigid rules rather than in being sensitive to human needs. Those with a grace orientation focus on what God has done and is doing for them. The result is a graciousness in their attitude toward life and people (Strommen, 1972).

The dilemma which the church faces is this: How do we reverse the treatment of Christian gays who sometimes feel treated like people left outside the church as strangers at the gate? How can we be honest with the truth while being grace oriented in the ways we respond to Christian gays who believe earnestly what research contradicts?

It is significant that Surgeon General Dr. C. Everett Koop who made no bones about his abhorrence of sexual promiscuity and consistently used the word "sodomy" when referring to homosexuality, nevertheless lobbied on their behalf and cared for them. He said, "I'm the Surgeon General for all the people and I'll meet them where they are. In addition, I've asked for compassion for them and for volunteers to go and care for them."

Though he never compromised his beliefs, no evangelical Christian is more appreciated by homosexuals (Yancey, 1997).

A Major Issue in Many Denominations

Gay activists want their point of view established in the church. Many believe that faith in Christ demands that they take up the cause of homosexual people because they have been hurt by moral and ecclesiastical strictures against homosexual practices. For some, nothing less than the survival of the faith is at stake. Some of these people are on national committees and boards of church bodies. Note what is happening.in my denomination, the Evangelical Lutheran Church in America (ELCA).

Some members of the Division for Outreach of the ELCA have been pressing for the ordination of practicing gays and lesbians as a "logical next step" to that of congregations extending hospitality to homosexuals. They view this as a necessary step in according equality to homosexuals.

A strong advocate of this position is Bishop Paul Egertson of the Southern California West Synod. He wants the Lutheran church to provide "liturgical blessings for gay/lesbian unions and permit congregations to choose openly gay ordained and lay ministers who are either single and celibate or coupled in a permanent, committed, monogamous, and blessed covenant." He feels so strongly this should be done that in his speech at Central Lutheran Church in Minneapolis, October 10, 1998, he was willing, among other things, to encourage that ecclesiastical disobedience be used as a stratagem by its advocates.

In another sector of the church an action was taken that evoked a strong negative reaction from pastors. The Lutheran Youth Organization (LYO) adopted a resolution at their 1997 gathering in New Orleans asking appropriate ELCA divisions to consider co-hosting a pre-gathering conference in the year 2000 for "gay, lesbian, and bisexual youth." The resolution also asked that programming address "the personal and faith issues affecting gay, lesbian, and bisexual youth." A flood of irate letters caused the leaders to postpone this action.

The incendiary nature of this topic of homosexuality is seen in the response of letters to the headquarters of the Evangelical Lutheran Church following its release of a document on human sexuality. A total of 2500 letters was received, most of them protesting its stand on homosexuality. This represented the largest number of letters ever received on any issue.

Debates in Many Denominations

The issue of homosexuality has precipitated debate in most Protestant denominations, leading Stanley Grenz, professor of theology and ethics at Caret/Regent College, Vancouver, to say, "The fundamental question now being debated is whether or not contemporary understandings of homosexuality demand that the church revise its long standing declaration that homosexual behavior is sinful" (Grenz 1998).

Concerted efforts are currently underway to get national assemblies of major denominations to legitimize the ordination of noncelibate homosexuals and to legitimize homosexual marriages.

Heated debates (amply reported in the *Christian Century* magazine) have occurred at denominational conventions of the United Methodists, Presbyterians (U.S.A.), United Church of Canada, The Mennonite Church, General Conference Mennonite Church, Central Conference of American Rabbis, and Episcopalians —with a growing division of opinion. Though most Protestant denominations have continued to maintain that homosexual clergy must remain celibate and that no gay marriages be performed or blessed, the issue is not settled. There are many who believe a time is coming when this issue will split their church.

It is significant that this near equal division of opinion among some Protestant denominations with respect to homosexuality is not shared by Christian churches outside the United States. In 1998 at the international meeting of Episcopal /Anglican leaders known as the Lambeth Conference, bishops from countries throughout the world voted 526 to 70 to endorse a resolution declaring homosexual behavior "incompatible with Scripture."

This decision was not welcomed by many of the Episcopal clergy in our country. Forty Episcopal bishops already are known to have ordained 140 gays and lesbians who live in committed relationships.

The Episcopal Diocese of Minnesota at its annual convention, October 29-31, 1999, passed a resolution that in part was a reaction to the position of the Lambeth Conference. This resolution states that the diocese includes, welcomes, and embraces gay, lesbian, bisexual, and transgender members. It specifies that this welcome includes the privilege of ordination and the blessing of relationships (*Duluth News Tribune*, 1999). A similar position was taken by the Episcopal Diocese of Colorado at its Denver conference in the spring of 2000.

The contrast between this position and that of the Lambeth Conference (which represents 80 million Anglicans), was noted by the current presiding bishop of the Episcopal Church in the United States, Frank Griswold:

> My own sense of things is that we are living with very different perspectives on human sexuality, grounded in very different ways of approaching the question theologically. Some see the Word most active in terms of Scripture and tradition, and others see the Word most active in terms of human experience and what's actually being lived by men and women in our congregations. My sense is that there is no way to reconcile those different perspectives (Griswold, 1998).

The current position of the Evangelical Lutheran Church in America is the one Griswold mentions first—identifying God's Word with Scripture and tradition. It is a position taken with a compassionate and inquiring attitude. Note these statements in an open letter from the ELCA bishops in 1998:

> We repudiate all words and acts of hatred toward gay and lesbian persons in our congregations and in our communities, and extend a caring welcome for gay and lesbian persons and their families. We invite gay and lesbian persons to join with other members of this church in mutual prayer and study of the issues that still divide us so that we may seek truth together (*An Open Letter from the Bishops of the Evangelical Lutheran Church in America*, March 22, 1998.)

The question remains before us. Should Christian churches continue to condemn homosexuality and reject homosexuals, or should they fully endorse the gay agenda?

Or is there a middle way?

Chapter Seven
WHAT DOES THE BIBLE SAY?

On this topic I can speak only as a pastor and not as a Biblical scholar. I can only share what has impressed me. The church has taught for centuries that homosexual practices are wrong in God's eyes. This stance is reinforced through the Biblical scholarship found in theologian Robert Gagnon's recent book, *The Bible and Homosexual Practices* , published in 2001 .

This book draws high praise from 15 internationally recognized Biblical scholars in America and Europe. They characterize the book as presenting the most erudite and thorough analysis of biblical texts available today on the issue of homosexual practices. Here is the argument of his book

"First, there is clear, strong, and credible evidence that the Bible unequivocally defines same-sex intercourse as sin. Second, there exist no valid hermeneutical arguments , derived from either general principles of biblical interpretation or contemporary scientific knowledge and experience, for overriding the Bible's authority on this matter. In sum, the Bible presents the anatomical, sexual, and procreative complementarity of male and female as clear and convincing proof of God's will for sexual unions. Even those who do not accept the revelatory authority of Scripture should be able to perceive the divine will through the visible testimony of the structure of creation. Thus, same-sex intercourse constitutes an inexcusable rebellion against the intentional design of the created order" (p.37).

He notes that early Judaism was unanimous in its rejection of homosexual conduct The same was true for Jewish authors who wrote during the centuries before and after the birth of Jesus. And the Apostle Paul writing in the New Testament identifies same-sex intercourse and unrestrained passion for such practices as sin. (Robert Gagnon ,2001)

The Christian Church's traditional condemnation of homosexuality is based on a handful of Bible passages.

"You shall not lie with a male as with a woman, it is an abomination" (Levitcus18:22)

"If a man lies with a male as with a woman, both of them have committed an abomination, they should be put to death; their blood is upon them" (Leviticus 20:13).

"Do you not know that wrong doers will not inherit the kingdom of God? Do not be deceived! Fornicators, idolaters, adulterers, male prostitutes, sodomites, thieves, the greedy, drunkards, revelers, robbers—none of these will inherit the kingdom of God. And this is what some of you used to be" (I Corinthians 6:9-11).

". . . the law is laid down not for the innocent but for the lawless and disobedient, for the godless and sinful, for the unholy and profane, for those who kill their father or mother, for murderers, fornicators, sodomites, slave traders, liars, perjurers, and whatever else is contrary to the sound teaching that conforms to the glorious gospel of the blessed God which he entrusted to me." (I Timothy1:10-11).

"For this reason God gave them up to degrading passions. Their women exchanged natural intercourse for unnatural, and in the same way also the men, giving up natural intercourse with women, were consumed with passion for one another. Men committed shameless acts with men and received in their own persons the due penalty for their errors" (Romans1:26-27; see the entire context, Romans1:18-23).

In the traditional approach these passages were understood according to their obvious meaning, a method of interpretation commended by Martin Luther.

Luther wrote, "No violence is to be done to the words of God, whether by man or angel; but [the Scriptures] are to be retained in their simplest meaning wherever possible, and to be understood in their grammatical and literal sense unless the context plainly forbids" (*The Babylonian Captivity of the Church,* Luther, 1909).

One more quote from Luther: "The Holy Spirit is the plainest writer and speaker in heaven and earth, therefore His words cannot have more than one, and that the very simplest, sense, which we call the literal, ordinary, natural sense. . . . It is much surer and safer to abide by the words in their simple sense"

(Answer to the Superchristian, Superspiritual, and Superlearned Book of Goat Emser).

If we interpret Leviticus 18:22 and Leviticus 20:13, in their literal and natural sense, we must conclude that God commands us to abstain from homosexuality.

Gagnon notes that Lev.18.22 ("You shall not lie with a male as with a woman") occurs in a larger context of forbidden sexual relations that primarily outlaws incest and also prohibits adultery, child sacrifice , and bestiality . These prohibitions continue to have universal validity in contemporary society. Only the prohibition against having sexual intercourse with a woman in her menstrual uncleanness (18.19) does not.

If we interpret 1 Corinthians 6:9-11 and 1 Timothy 1:10 in their obvious and natural way we will conclude that we should avoid those acts forbidden there (which include greed and lying). According to these texts, homosexuality is a behavior God does not favor. This is reiterated in Romans 1:26-27 where same-sex intercourse (both male and female) are identified as an outcome of failing to honor God as God.

Again Gagnon notes that in Leviticus 20, where penalties are prescribed for many of the forbidden acts of Leviticus, in chapters 18 and19, the word "abomination" is applied only and specifically to sexual intercourse between males (20.13) .In short, in the entire Holiness Code—indeed, in the entire priestly corpus of the Tetrateuch—the only forbidden act to which the designation "abomination" is specific ally attached is homosexual intercourse.

To me the word "abomination" is a harsh word. I wince when I hear it used to club and viciously condemn homosexuals. Nevertheless, I recognize that this word is in the text. For that reason it requires a stretch of the imagination to say that homosexual behavior is another expression of God's creation—an activity which He can bless and honor. One is faced by the issue— How authoritative is God's Word? Does one take seriously what is written in Scripture?

A literal interpretation of the Holiness Code as found in Leviticus 18 and 20 would not be included in Luther's interpretation of Scripture. These passages prescribe the death penalty for men lying together in a homosexual relationship, idolatry, cursing one's parents, adultery, certain forms of incest, being a medium or wizard, blasphemy, or murder. They also condemn the eating of pork, wearing two kinds of clothing, sabbath breaking, as well as requiring circumcision.

These requirements of Moses were addressed in a speech by Peter on behalf of the Gentiles to whom he had brought the message of salvation. Addressing the council assembled in Jerusalem he said: "Why are you putting God to the test by placing on the neck of the disciples a yoke that neither our ancestors nor we have been able to bear. On the contrary we believe that we will be saved through the grace of the Lord Jesus, just as they will" (Acts 15:10-11).

By way of summary to what the council concluded after deliberating this issue, James the leader said, "We should not trouble those Gentiles who are turning to God, but we should write to them to abstain only from things polluted by idols and from fornication and from whatever has been strangled and from blood" (Acts 15:19-20).

This action set aside the requirements of the Mosaic Code. It supported the theology of Paul who appealed to the Galatians not to be entangled again with the yoke of bondage. His message was this: "We know that a person is justified not by the works of the law but through faith in Jesus Christ" (Galations.2:16).

James, writing in his epistle, underscored how imperative it was in the moral atmosphere of the first century to include the prohibition of fornication. He saw it as necessary in order to guard the Christian life from sexual defilement. Added support is found in the burning language of St. Paul in 1 Corinthians 6:15-20 and 1 Thessalonians 4:3-6. He identifies the terrible risks to which Christian morality was exposed, a risk that was enhanced by the fact that a heathen view of impurity was extremely lax throughout the Roman empire

Reinterpreting Passages on Homosexuality

Some biblical scholars are reinterpreting the scriptural passages that deal with homosexuality so they do not condemn homosexual behavior among consenting adults. I am not persuaded

They point out that there are some legitimate questions about the meaning of the Greek words used to refer to homosexuals in the New Testament passages quoted above: *malakoi* and *arsenokoitai*. Do they apply to all forms of homosexual behavior, or to male prostitutes or sexual acts with boys? Biblical scholars will continue to debate this question.

Gagnon says the following about these two Greek words. "I have translated *malakoi*, which literally means "the soft ones" as effeminate males who play the sexual role of female; and *arsenokoitai* , which literally means "male bedders", as males who take other males to bed. Advocates of homosexuality among Christians offer other readings.

In I Corinthians 6.9, *malakoi* are sandwiched in between adulterers, people who commit an act of immoral sexual intercourse, *and arsenokoitai,* people who have something to do with an immoral act of same-sex intercourse. That *arsenokoitai* refers to same-sex intercourse is strengthened by its pairing with *malakoi* (Gagnon, 2001, p.308, 16).

I sat in an all-day seminar sponsored by the Faith and Life . Forum which was advertised as being a "model of moral delibera-tion in which all points of view are deliberately represented." Unfortunately the forum focused on only one point of view. I listened to a most engaging presentation by an New Testament professor retranslating Romans 1:26-31. His thesis was this: "This passage is not about sex but about injustice." He then proceeded to explain how the Greek had been incorrectly translated showing how his translation should be viewed as the correct one.

I reflected on the adequacy of the translation to which he made reference. The New Revised Standard Version of 1989 was revised for three reasons: 1) the acquisition of still older biblical manuscripts; 2) further investigation of linguistic features of the text; and, 3) changes in preferred English usage. Instead of one person there was a committee of translators who based their work on the most recent edition of the Greek New Testament prepared by an interconfessional and international committee. I saw no reason why I should I set aside their translation for the one he proposed, especially when his purpose in revising the passage was seemingly to substantiate a certain point of view.

Though the seminar presented a retranslation of biblical passages that condemn homosexuality it failed to make provision for a rejoinder. Rather it provided a platform for the gay-lesbian position while giving only a minimal opportunity for a contrasting position. It failed to present the contrasting points of view that stimulate discussion and facilitate thought on facets of homosexuality troubling to those grappling with this issue.

The position given visibility at this workshop was the position being advocated by many gays and lesbians, namely that one is born a homosexual, that it is an orientation that cannot be changed, that people should accept it as normal, and it should be celebrated as part of God's creation.

The underlying assumption of those holding such a position seems to be this: If everyone adopts this value orientation, gay-bashing and the horrible treatment accorded known gays will be eliminated. Therefore this point of view should be made part of the curriculum in both our public schools and programs of religious education. If children are helped to view homosexuality as normal, then as they grow older, condemnation and discrimination of homosexuals will largely disappear.

This position is currently being held by many intelligent and devout Christians in the Lutheran church and most other denominations. They are biblically oriented Christians who are conscious of Christ's command to "love one another as I have loved you." Out of concern for homosexuals, they want to abandon the church's traditional position.

This philosophical position could be adopted as the official position of major denominations. That is what some advocates want. It can be assumed that as educators, pastors, laity, theologians, and policy makers come to accept the position that gays represent another expression of God's creation it will gradually become church policy.

Studies in the field of innovation and change have established the fact that in the absence of intellectual opposition, an opposing notion will gradually come to be absorbed into the culture. It will be accepted by degrees, by dint of constant pressure on one side and constant retreat on the other, until the day when it suddenly becomes the church's official position.

In addition to those retranslating the Bible passages dealing with homosexuality, some theologians and church leaders are reinterpreting these passages to mean something different from the church's traditional position.

As a result of their efforts the historic position of the church is being fiercely attacked. One such theologian is John McNeill in his book, *Taking a Chance on God: Liberating Theology for Gays, Lesbians, and Their Lovers, Families, and Friends.* He says, "We must ask ourselves which of the church's values we continue to want, respect, and love; in other words, which values are compatible with who we are and are not destructive of our dignity as persons" (McNeill, 1988).

Theologians, some gay and lesbian and some not, are reinterpreting biblical passages to remove their condemnation of homosexuality. Some are saying that the Apostle Paul was simply wrong in what he said. Peter Gomes (1996) a homosexual pastor at Harvard University, argues in his book, *The Good Book: Reading the Bible with Mind and Heart,* that the Christian church has arrived at a more enlightened position than what the Bible says about slavery and women. Therefore, he says, we should do the same with respect to homosexuality.

Gomes suggests that the Bible supports slavery and the second class treatment of women. But does it? We are aware of how Christ's treatment of women broke with the customs of his day and how Paul's treatment of Onesimus, a runaway slave, pointed to a new day in how slaves were to be viewed.

It is significant that the preaching and teaching of Christ and his apostles did not address social issues but rather focused on people's relationship to Jesus Christ. They chose not to address social ills of the day such as men's treatment of women, the centuries old trafficking in slaves, the cruel treatment of prisoners, the use of crucifixion, or the wide-spread abuses of a corrupt government headed by the Herod family. Their message focused solely on a faith relationship with Jesus Christ. As a result this message has permeated society like a yeast and profoundly influenced how these social ills are viewed today. Paul pointed to such changes when he wrote: "As many of you as were baptized into Christ have clothed yourself with Christ. There is no longer Jew or Greek, there is no longer slave or free, there is no longer male or female; for all of you are one in Christ Jesus" (Galations 3:27-28). His words announced a new day with respect to how women, slaves, and ethnic groups were to be viewed.

And this is how many Christians have interpreted the Scriptures. The effect of their interpretation is shown in the changes taking place in how slavery has come to be viewed. These changes are noted by Charles Greenidge, Honorary Director, Anti-Slavery Society in his comprehensive article on slavery in the *Encyclopedia Britannica*. He writes:

> Slavery was a fundamental element of the old Roman constitution. It could not be expected that a radical alteration could be suddenly wrought either in the social system which was in harmony with it, or even in the general ideas which had grown up under its influence. However, the rise of Christianity in the Roman world improved the condition of the slave. The sentiments it created were not only favorable to humane treatment but were the germs out of which its entire liberation was destined to arise.

> In the first centuries, the church encouraged the emancipation of individual slaves and the redemption of captives. Its influence is to be seen in the legislation of the Christian emperors which softened some of its harshest features. . . .A new process of manumission was established to be performed in the churches through the intervention of the ministers of religion. It was provided that clerics could at any time by mere expression of will liberate their slaves (Greenidge, Vol. 20, pp. 777-778).

We know that down through the centuries there were Christians who supported slavery and those who found a scriptural basis for opposing it. This division of opinion was notably true in the early 1800s when congregations in the United States were taking an active role in the peace and reform movements. According to Paul Kuenning in his book, *The Rise and Fall of American Lutheran Pietism,* the movement to abolish human slavery was "far and away the overriding moral reform issue of the day. It was the 'question of questions'" (Kuenning, 1988).

Resisting this reform movement were churches in the South who felt there was a scriptural basis for supporting the practice of slavery. The strong difference of opinion in that day would be comparable to the division of opinion that is occurring within denominations on the issue of homosexuality.

If one differs with Gomes on the issue of slavery, one must agree with his observation that leaders in the church have chosen to reinterpret Paul's statement that women should not teach in the church or have authority over men. The reinterpretation of Paul's requirement clearly reflects the social changes of today. But the issue of women being given leadership in the church is not parallel to the issue of homosexuality. One is a social issue—the other is a moral issue.

More serious, however, is the reinterpretation being given Christ's clear statements on divorce. It has effects in the lives of people that differ radically from the effects of allowing women to teach in the church. Here I make reference to the long-lasting negative impact divorce is shown to have on children. One wonders what justification can be given for the casual disregard of the wisdom contained in Christ's prohibition of divorce (except in the case of adultery)?

Those who reinterpret certain select passages of Scripture believe that what is written in the Bible about homosexuality does not apply to today's situation. Some biblical scholars in making their reinterpretation go a step further and actually contend that a writer was wrong in what he wrote. That is what Walter Wink, professor of biblical interpretation at Auburn Theological Seminary, says about Paul's statements regarding homosexuality. In his book, *Homosexuality and Christian Faith*, Wink writes: "Where the Bible mentions homosexual behavior at all, it clearly condemns it. The issue is precisely whether that biblical judgment is correct. . . . If now new evidence is in on the phenomenon of homosexuality, are we not obligated—no, free—to reevaluate the whole issue in the light of all the available data and decide what is right under God?" (Wink, 1999).

I wrote to Professor Wink and asked what this new evidence was. He was not able to supply this new evidence in his answering letter.

A Case for the Church's Traditional Position

It is significant that the church from its earliest days has rejected same-sex practices. The initial target of the Patristic church with respect to homosexuality was pederasty, men having sex with boys. During the Middle Ages the target was same-sex among the clergy and those in monasteries. To address what had become widespread, the church officially condemned the practice of homosexuality at its Third Lateran Council of 1179. A review of history shows that in each era of the church, Christian moralists have rejected same-sex practices.

Has the case been made for change on biblical grounds? Clearly the church's traditional position is being challenged and even rejected by a number of articulate voices. But current scholarship still makes a strong case for the traditional position.

Stanley Grenz in his book, *Welcoming but not Affirming*, says, "The church today appears to be faced with two seemingly contrary alternatives: Do we maintain the traditional ecclesiastical opposition to same-sex intercourse and to homosexual unions? Or do we conclude that the time has come to revise our stance on this moral issue?" (Grenz, 1998).

Grenz analyzes the arguments of those theologians wanting to reinterpret the church's historic position and concludes: "Scholars who propose that the church accept committed same-sex relationships have yet to produce a sufficient basis for revising the traditional belief that the biblical writers condemned homosexual conduct. The supposed naturalness of a person's same-sex preference does not set aside the biblical call to engage in genital sexual expression exclusively within monogamous heterosexual marriage" (Grenz, 1999).

A well-known contemporary theologian, Wolfhart Pannenberg, professor of systematic theology at the University of Munich takes a strong position against theologians who contest the historic position of the Christian church. In an article entitled "You Shall Not Lie with a Male," he concludes by saying:

> Those who would press the church to change the norm of her teaching on this question must understand that they press the church toward schism. For a church which allows itself to be pushed to regard homosexual activity as no longer a departure from the biblical norm and to recognize homosexual partnerships as a form of personal relationship equivalent to marriage would no longer stand on the foundation of the Scripture but rather in opposition to its unanimous witness. A church that takes such a step has thereby ceased to be an evangelical church in the tradition of the Lutheran Reformation (Pannenberg, 1996).

The council of the Evangelical Church in Germany, through a task force which it established, published a position paper on homosexuality and the church entitled "Living With Tensions." I read this document with interest because here is a church body from which has come respected theologians and biblical scholars.

The document argues that debate in the church on homosexuality must follow theological lines. "Even the majority view of the phenomenon of homosexuality in the human science today cannot be considered to have any normative significance for a theological assessment" (p. 9).

In a discussion of the statements in I Corinthians 6:9 and I Timothy 1:10 the paper notes that Paul having referred to "homosexual offenders" then refers to certain members of the Corinthian congregation as those who"used to be" like this but have been "washed clean" by the name of Jesus Christ and the Spirit of God (I Corinthians 6:11). The paper adds, "So Paul bases his view on the experience that baptism can change people even with reference to their sexual behavior" (p. 15).

With respect to the biblical statement carrying the greatest theological weight, namely Romans 1:26 ff, the paper says, "We should not conclude that Paul is speaking here only about people with heterosexual inclinations who have switched over to homosexual practices. It is not a matter of particular individuals or groups, but a form of behavior which Paul considers a fundamental distortion of the relationship to God" (p.15).

The paper also notes that love in the Old Testament and especially in the New Testament is the quintessence of the will of God. Hence, a relationship needs to be established between the commandment of love, as the essence of God's saving will for humankind, and the question of an ethically responsible expression of homosexuality. The tension for church, however, is that an emphasis on love "does not change the fact that no biblical statements exist which place homosexuality in a positive relation to the will of God" (p.17).

It is significant that God gives the following admonition in connection with his great command to "love your neighbor as yourself" , Note these words from Leviticus 19.17-18.

"Do not hate your brother in your heart. Rebuke your neighbor frankly so you will not share in his guilt. Do not seek revenge or bear a grudge against one of your people. But love your neighbor as yourself. I am the Lord." (NIV)

Here we see that love does not always refrain from disagreeing with our neighbor neither does it justify being hateful and cruel with one's neighbor. There are times when love motivates us to speak up and challenge the actions of our neighbor. The issue of homosexuality can be a case in point.

The paper proposes that homosexual people who understand their inclinations as either an unchangeable characteristic or as a defect in the development should be allowed to live with this interpretation without insisting that their view is valid for all. Furthermore, it insists that people with homosexual leanings are entitled to pastoral counseling, a priority task for Christian congregations and churches. Whether this counseling is used must remain the free choice of homosexual people (pp.32-33).

Faithfulness to the Bible

At this point it may be beneficial to remind ourselves of the purpose of the Bible. From an evangelical perspective, the Bible is not primarily a rule book to govern every aspect of our conduct. Its main purpose is to bring people—all people, heterosexual and homosexual—into a saving and transforming relationship with Jesus Christ. As followers of Jesus and members of his body, we are part of a new community. "As many of you as were baptized into Christ have clothed yourself with Christ. There is no longer Jew or Greek, no longer slave or free, there is no longer male or female, for all of you are one in Christ Jesus" (Galations 3:27-28).

We speak of the God's word as presenting both the Law and the Gospel. For Christians the Law (according to Luther) teaches us what we should and should not do to lead a God-pleasing life. The Law thus is a guide. The power to live according to the Law comes from the Gospel.

In the current debate on what the Bible says about homosexuality, those who hold to the historic interpretation want to be faithful to the Scriptures and the tradition of the church and are convinced that these should not be overturned without compelling theological reasons.

Those who wish to reinterpret the church's position are doing that out of love for homosexuals and the desire to protect them from injustice and rejection. They are well-intentioned, but before we accept their agenda we need to look at its implications for the church.

Chapter Eight

SHOULD THE CHURCH
ADOPT THE GAY AGENDA?

As we have seen in the last chapter, there is a concerted effort to force Christian churches to adopt the gay agenda. If a Christian denomination were to change its position and adopt the gay agenda (including ordination of non-celibate gays, blessing of same-sex marriages), it would need to address the following issues.

1. More evidence than is now available would have to be found to justify setting aside the historic position of the Christian and Jewish faith communities and not least, the convictions of today's Christian church throughout the world.

2. The leaders responsible for such a change would need to explain why they oppose current programs and therapies that help homosexuals wishing to change their orientation.

3. Why is the need to reinterpret scripture so great that the church must risk schism?

4. Pastors would need to explain to their people why passages on homosexuality in the New Testament no longer have their traditional meaning.

5. Pastors who adopt the assumptions that God has created some to be homosexuals, that this orientation is irreversible for some, and that it should be viewed as normal would need to find a rationale for adopting as truth something which has not been established as true. The strongest evidence available today indicates that these assumptions are false.

6. The church would need to accept responsibility for becoming a social factor that significantly influences persons, especially youth, toward a homosexual orientation.

7. Why does the church need to change its teachings in order to welcome gays and lesbians?

Conclusions Based on Available Evidence

As we look back at all the evidence from the most reliable sources, what conclusions can be derived? I suggest the following theses for open discussion.

1. The evidence from the Bible is this: homosexual behavior is not encouraged for God's people. The position paper of the German Lutheran Church states, "No biblical statements exist which place homosexuality in a positive relation to the will of God." The Bible identifies boundaries that have been established for our good as well as the good of children and families.

2. There is no credible research evidence to establish homosexuality as an "innate, genetically determined aspect of the human body." Furthermore, there is ample evidence that the orientation is reversible for some.

3. The best explanation for the emergence of a homosexual orientation is that it is caused by many factors, most of which are outside the control of the persons involved. Therefore people in the church, rather than discrediting or condemning homosexuals, should be the first to support ways of reaching out to them in love and making available help in bringing about change for those dissatisfied with their orientation.

4. There are people who for unknown reasons cannot change their sexual orientation. They need to be accepted in the church either as people struggling with an unwanted orientation or as people fully satisfied with their orientation.

5. As a church we need to join hands with those in the scientific community who are seeking to bring sense to this subject and who are seeking to discover the most successful ways of bringing about a reorientation. A ready resource is available in a considerable number of social scientists who do not agree with the political positions taken by their professional organization on the subject of homosexuality.

6. The evidence is clear that some homosexuals can change. This message should be made public so that persons struggling with this issue can know there is an option. They should know that there are effective secular and religious approaches to the healing of homosexuality.

In its discussions of homosexuality, the Evangelical Lutheran Church in America so far has muted two basic considerations.

One is that of making provision for those who wish to change their orientation. The other is giving ex-gays a chance to voice their opinions when the issue of homosexuality is being discussed in the church.

Norman Williamsen, a volunteer at the Denver Churchwide Assembly of the ELCA in 1999, noticed that when the issue of practicing homosexuals was considered, no discussion of faith-based reorientation therapies was offered. He wrote a letter to the ELCA Church Council requesting that in their continuing discussions of homosexuality they give equal time to listening to what "healed homosexuals" have to say.

An illustration of the help that can be given by the church has been launched by the Jewish Orthodox community. An outreach organization called JONAH has been established to assist homosexual men and women seeking to change their sexual orientation. According to the group's director, Rabbi Samuel Rosenberg, the name Jonah is an acronym for "Jews Offering New Alternatives to Homosexuality."

Rosenberg adds that "Jewish ethics require us to offer assistance to those who struggle with homosexuality and to understand how to help men and women with same-sex attractions. In today's society it is important to offer solutions to problems, otherwise, one becomes part of the problem" (Rosenberg, 2000)

Special Consideration for Young People

I believe the church should have a special concern for adolescents who think they are homosexual. Faced with fears, bewilderment, and puzzlement regarding their future, they find little help in most churches. If they voice their suspicion to a school counselor, they are likely to hear they are gay and cannot change their orientation. They will be encouraged to join a gay organization and find the support of others similarly oriented. There their orientation may become largely fixed.

My concern is for the young adolescent male because the issue of homosexuality is raised at a relatively early age. In the 1998 study of 882 dissatisfied homosexuals, respondents were asked to identify the time when they first became aware of homosexual tendencies. The average age of these reports was 14 years.

Sixty percent of these said they experienced their first homosexual contact when they were a child at the average age of 11. Their estimate of the age of those older persons who made homosexual contacts with them was 17 (Byrd, 1998). Clearly, the issue of homosexuality is very real for many early adolescents.

According to Satinover, boys who have never known the encircling arms of a loving father develop an intense, nonsexual attachment to older boys whom they admire. When puberty sets in, sexual urges—which can attach themselves to any object, especially in males—rise to the surface. They combine with an already intense need for masculine intimacy and warmth to develop into homosexual crushes (Satinover, 1996).

A pastoral counselor, Clinton R. Jones, who has worked with at least 2000 gays or lesbians, describes adolescents in his book, *Youth Considers: What About Homosexuality?* He gives an account of how adolescents who come to him to discuss their homosexual feelings respond. His description resembles the one given by Carolyn Riehl in 1998 of the feelings experienced by 35 ELCA pastors when first discovering that they were homosexual or lesbian. Jones writes,

> "Can you help?" That often is one of the first questions a high school boy asks me in his first interview. Such a conference is usually traumatic—so difficult for the boy and none too easy for the counselor who sees that the boy is nervous, tense, uncomfortable, even frightened; he hardly knows what to say or how to describe what may be in his mind and heart. The boy is in pain, and it is pain which has brought him to the counselor's office—the pain of knowing or fearing he has homosexual feelings (Jones, 1972).

What the adolescent boy does not know is that such feelings tend to characterize ages 8 through 14, often referred to as the "normal homosexual period." If he is slow in moving out of this period, the boy assumes his fate is fixed—that he is a homosexual. This assumption is encouraged when schools provide clubs to support and establish gays and lesbians in their orientation.

Some Adolescents Need Early Prevention

Adolescent males need to hear that 1) they are not necessarily gay; or, 2) if they are predominately gay, they can change. They need to hear that there is an option, that a homosexual orientation is not inevitable, that they are at a prime time in life to stop its development in their lives. The executive director for NARTH had this to say about early prevention:

> The future is in prevention. What can be done for male children between the ages of 3 and 14 can save what is later difficult to overcome.
>
> Clients who have been in a gay lifestyle for many years say that as adults they feel almost "hard-wired" into unwanted same-sex behaviors. Today, these men deeply regret not having had help during boyhood when they were defensively detaching from their fathers, their male peers, and their own masculine selves.
>
> Just a few months working with a prehomosexual child can produce results that would take years with an adult homosexual.
>
> I believe the future of reparative therapy is in early diagnosis and prevention (Nicolosi, 1999).

Those who are especially "at risk" are those showing these characteristics at an early age: alienation from same sex peers; loneliness, anxiety, depression, gender-identity confusion; and a poor relationship with their father. More extreme evidences can be noted in such statements as "I want to be a girl," or showing a fascination with women's clothing, or demonstrating an effeminacy in mannerisms, gestures, and play.

Unfortunately, there are few long term studies on childhood intervention designed to establish a male identity. But Nicolosi, whose life's work has focused on homosexuality, has worked with parents whose sons have evidenced the above characteristics. In one of his lectures he reported the following outcomes of his work with parents whose children evidence gender-identity problems.

- Decreased effeminacy
- Increased self-esteem and more adventuresome behavior
- Increased maturity and being less occupied with self
- Diminished anxiety and depression
- Popularity with other boys
- Contentment with being a boy

His appeal is to the parental team that they be committed to their child's best interests of being "happy to be a boy." Mother needs to reflect esteem for masculinity, and father needs to accept a vital role in the life of the son.

He proposes the following pro-active steps.

• Intervening, giving a clear affirming, consistent gender message: "You are a boy. It's good to be a boy."

• Correcting with gentle disapproval. "That's what girls do—but you're a boy."

• Encouraging male friendships and activities with boyhood peers, relatives, neighbors, coaches, teachers.

• Avoiding excessive pressure to bring about conformity or on the other hand, becoming immobilized with respect to action.

When a boy is comfortable as a male, he is more likely to be heterosexual (Nicolosi, 2000)

Adolescents need to learn where they can go to cope with this issue—to someone who has both theological and psychological expertise, someone who can help them turn in the direction they want to go. An excellent resource for those working with youth is the book *An Ounce of Prevention: Preventing the Homosexual Condition in Today's Youth* by Don Schmierer (1998). It is a well-researched book that gives solid information and direction regarding what can be done to minimize environmental influences toward homosexuality.

Adolescents Need Heterosexual Role Models

To develop a strong gender identity and heterosexual orientation, a boy needs strong, positive heterosexual role models. In their formative years confirmands can be especially influenced by their pastor. For many, the pastor epitomizes how the Christian life should be lived. The pastor's unique position of power and influence has an unconscious shaping influence on an adolescent's life.

For this reason I am opposed to the ordination of noncelibate homosexuals. This position is based on a finding that alarmed our staff at Search Institute when we reviewed the results of a study of high school students A description of the study is found in *Five Cries of Youth* (Strommen, 1993).

We discovered that the belief orientation of three professional trainers influenced the religious measures of the youth they trained *even though God talk was never permitted.* The religious scores of youth trained by an agnostic declined more than could be accounted for by chance. The scores of those trained by a nominal church member remained the same. The scores of those trained under a psychologist clergyman increased significantly. Here was striking evidence that a well-liked leader unconsciously influences the religious life and participation of those being led even though religious language is not involved.

The position paper for the German Lutheran Church recognizes the environmental effect of persons in power who represent homosexuality.

> Since the sexual leanings of young people evolve in the interplay between their disposition (which can be influenced) and their own decisions about their behavior, the influential effect of the socially recognized educative authorities also becomes important (Position Paper, p.40).

This social factor is identified in the report given by researchers at the University of Chicago following their extensive study of *Sex in America:*

> Having identified several distinct orientations, we then demonstrated the extent to which they are socially organized—that is, the extent to which their occurrence may be predicted by the presence or absence of specific master statuses. This general finding provides an important link in what has been the main argument of this book—namely, that the ways in which people understand sexuality, and hence the behaviors that they engage in and expect from their partners, are heavily conditioned by the social groups to which they belong (Laumann, et al. 1994).

> Historian John Boswell In his book, *Christianity, Social Tolerance, and Homosexuality: Gay People in Western Europe,* estimates that the number of homosexuals in Athens exceeded the number of heterosexuals. Saint John Chrysostom averred that in fourth-century Antioch, heterosexuals were in the minority. In a fourteenth century German village of 3000 people, the inquisitor Jacques Fournier estimated that half the men were homosexuals.

(pp.54-55) It would certainly be a stretch of one's imagination to conclude that such large numbers of men practicing homosexual behavior in these various cities were born that way.

Rather, it is more reasonable to conclude that the widespread practice of homosexuality found to exist iin the early cities of Athens, Rome, Thessaly, Ionia, Crete and Sparta can best be attributed to the fact these men were influenced to adopt homosexual practices when young males. As "darling boys" they were the erotic object of older men. Social environment is a significant factor.

Without question the stand of a faith community can be important in deterring the development of homosexuality in young adolescents. The modeling by a pastor can be an important factor.

What is true regarding the potential influence of noncelibate pastors would apply also to people in leadership positions or serving as youth leaders. When they are well liked and influential, they can communicate their values and philosophy of life unconsciously.

My secondary objective in writing this book is to deter as many adolescents as possible from a life of homosexuality. This means encouraging fathers to be fathers to their sons, providing information to adolescents troubled by homosexual leanings, identifying counselors who can assist in reducing the power of homosexual thoughts, and countering the efforts of schools to route adolescents into homosexual clubs. Efforts need to be made to reduce rather than increase the environmental pressures that encourage youth towards homosexuality.

Because of my concern for youth and because of the other issues raised in this chapter, I believe there are sound, compassionate reasons for insisting that the church should not uncritically and wholly accept the gay agenda. I believe there is a better way—better for homosexuals and their families and better for the church. I will outline this "middle way" in the concluding chapter.

Chapter Nine

SEARCHING FOR A MIDDLE GROUND

Throughout this book we have been searching for a middle ground regarding homosexuals in the church—a middle ground between condemnation and rejection, on the one hand, and adoption of the gay agenda on the other.

The church needs a position that is focused on ministry or pastoral care as opposed to judgment. Christ has called us to serve, minister, not simply judge.

In my opinion, we cannot identify ourselves as a church of Word and Sacrament if we adopt a theoretical position that is not true, that requires an alteration of Scripture, and that denies convincing research evidence. A position is needed that is open to the realities described in both Scripture and scientific research.

A Dialectic Approach to Ministry

For me, a necessary position requires a dialectic in which two seeming opposites are held in tension. Biblical truths are often understood this way. To illustrate, we believe that Christ was both human and divine—the coexistence of two opposites, We are familiar with the formulation: *simul justus et peccator* —that one is simultaneously a sinner and justified. Again we have two opposites being held in tension.

In the dialectic I propose, one polarity centers in the overwhelming call of God to love one another, to welcome the homosexual person as Christ would do.The other polarity centers in the conviction that homosexuality does not represent God's will for humankind, that it cannot be regarded as part of God's continuing creation. This dialectical position is faithful both to the Scriptures and God's call to love one another as God loves us.

Some may have trouble with this position, thinking that we as Christians are obligated to condemn homosexuals as sinners. If we choose to condemn people for homosexuality, then we need to condemn people for other sins strongly condemned in Scripture such as marrying after divorce (Matthew 19:9), ignoring the sick, naked, imprisoned, or strangers (Matthew 25:34-36), living in luxury and ignoring the poor (James 5:1), defrauding laborers (James 5:4), centering ones life in the acquisition of wealth (Ephesians 5:5), nurturing hate or an unforgiving spirit (I John 2:9)—the list can go on. Romans 2:1 reminds us that in passing judgment upon another, we condemn ourselves. Why? "There is none who is righteous, not even one" (Romans 3:11).

Pastor Roland Wells, makes this point clear in a paper entitled: *Toward a Biblical, Pastoral Teaching on Homosexuality.* He writes:

> "Most of our congregations have people who trust in Christ, but still deal with alcoholism. Some are "recovering", some are still "practicing". Week by week we minister to both. Indeed, a pastor may work with the family, offer resources, counsel the co-dependent spouse.,etc. But that alcoholic is still a member of the church".

"The man that sits down the pew struggles with coveteousness. The woman behind him struggles with bearing false-witness. The man behind her is struggling with the possibility of adultery in his marriage-grown-cold. Each of these people needs to clearly hear God's Word, *both* law and gospel. Each one will be saved by grace alone, each one will only be changed by the loving touch of the Word. Each needs to be called to repentance and faith. Each needs to be called away from sin and into freedom. Perhaps they will fall; but they all need the same thing. They need to hear the Word, repent from sin, and be called to faith."

So it is for those who struggle with homosexuality. Our preaching must include loving guidance to those who struggle this way.

The dialectic I propose enables the church to avoid being caught in the polarization where one shouts at the other and condemns what the other is doing or fails to do. It enables Christians to live in the sense of being under the authority of Scripture while demonstrating love to a much maligned people.

Sin always separates. The far right and far left justify their positions by judgment not ministry. They remain separate and accuse one another of being at fault

A ministry of the gospel, a theology of the cross, understands the tension that exists between Christ and culture. It teaches that all believers, though accountable for our sins, are yet declared righteous through Christ's redemptive action. It is within this dialectic that we can live and work.

Charting a Middle Ground

First, the church at all levels should continue to clearly and forcefully reject condemnation of homosexuals and acts of discrimination and injustice. Instead, we should be both a welcoming church, inviting homosexuals to be a part of the fellowship of believers—both homosexuals who are dissatisfied with their orientation and those who are satisfied with it as is.

We should provide in the congregation a welcome that is supportive and encouraging, free of rejection and discrimination. This means becoming creative in establishing new patterns of welcoming, including help for heterosexuals to overcome their negative attitudes toward homosexuals. In our churches we should care for homosexuals, welcome them, encourage them in the work of the church, help them when they are sick, accept those who are believers as brothers and sisters in the body of Christ.

Second, on the basis of the research summarized in this book, we should reject the gay agenda that maintains that all homosexuals are born that way, that they can never change, that a gay lifestyle should be affirmed and encouraged as normal and desirable.

Third, free discussion of the issues relating to homosexuality should be encouraged throughout the churches. This needs to be carried out in a respectful manner, with all parties given full access to the debate. All attempts to stifle or to limit the discussion to one perspective should be resisted.

This means, among other things, that the best research regarding the causes of homosexuality and the possibility of a change in orientation should be widely disseminated. Information on reorientation therapies should be available in our churches, and ex-gays should be allowed to tell their stories. The risks of a promiscuous homosexual lifestyle should be talked about openly.

I hope this book will help to provide reliable resources for such a discussion.

Fourth, as people bound by the Word of God, we should continue to study the Bible together, making every effort to hear what God is saying to us through that Word. No matter what our present position, we should be open to change our minds when we have been wrong.

It is imperative that we as the church of Jesus Christ do not acquiesce into adopting moral values of our culture that conflict with the Bible. If we simply follow the lead of our society, we become what H. Richard Niebuhr called "cultural Protestants, those who feel no great tension between the social norms and the Gospel" (Niebuhr, 1951).

Fifth, the church should continue to hold up committed, heterosexual marriage as God's ideal (recognizing that singleness is also a God-pleasing calling). In doing so, we are remaining faithful to the Bible and to the tradition of the Christian church. By doing so we may influence people, especially young people, away from a homosexual lifestyle and toward a heterosexual family life.

Seen from the point of view of the Christian faith, marriage and the family are the social models for the cohabitation of people as far as sexuality and generative activities are concerned. According to the position paper of the German Lutheran Church, "Marriage as an institution must remain the preserve of hetero-sexual couples" (p.30).

The rationale given by the German position paper is this: "Blessing is the assurance of God's support which, when it relates to a particular situation in life also includes the aspect of God's consent. The act of blessing cannot and must not be the means of achieving church or social recognition" (p.44).

Sixth, we need to exercise special concern for young people in our churches. This means providing a safe, nonjudgmental forum where they can receive reliable teaching about biblical morality and about sexual orientation and the possibility of its being changed.

We also need to provide youth, especially young males, with healthy role models. This may include mentoring or "Big Brother" programs for fatherless boys. This need for sound role models also leads me to oppose the ordaining into the ministry of practicing homosexuals.

Seventh, we should also be a transforming church, helping those dissatisfied with their homosexual orientation to seek change. We can do this by providing love, affirmation, counseling, and support groups. We can make available to pastors lists of trained therapists and provide financial aid to those who want therapy but cannot afford it.

We also need to admit that there are many heterosexuals in our churches who have negative, hate-filled, discriminatory attitudes toward homosexuals. They, too, are in need of transformation toward becoming more loving, gracious followers of Jesus Christ.

Eighth, because there is so much to learn about this complex phenomenon, we in the church ought to support and study research that seeks a greater understanding of homosexuality, its causes, and the possibilities of sexual reorientation.

This is the outline of the search for a middle ground for the church: it is a ministry model. I believe such a ministry model is faithful both to the Scriptures and our Christian tradition, and to the Lord who calls us to love one another as God has loved us and to live in peace and unity as members of the body of Christ.

EPILOGUE

The search for a middle ground becomes a practical issue when a congregation is asked to become a Reconciling in Christ congregation or a Transforming congregation. It is at such times that a free and open discussion is needed which respects the opinions of all. But this quality of interchange is made difficult not only by the context of America's social and political correctness but also by the differing perceptions of homosexuality held by church members.

Some equate the issue of homosexuality with racial discrimination or the past treatment of women. For them the debate is a justice issue.

Others view homosexuality as a human rights issue and consider the church's traditional position as nothing more than "old fashioned."

Some largely view attempts to arrive at a different relationship with homosexuals as an aggressive, liberal agenda.

Still others put the discussion of homosexuality in the context of biblical theology. These people are at a loss when respected leaders of the church provide new interpretations of traditional beliefs held by the church.

One purpose of this book is to draw attention to the issues that should be freely discussed regarding the issue of homosecuality in the church. These discussions should take place in an atmosphere of freedom without fear of intimidation or ridicule. One should be free to take differing positions on this issue without being labelled a bigot. Differences should be freely discussed knowing that the love of God is inclusive, his forgiveness is redemptive, and life in a spiritual community is empowering.

In all of the discussions, there should be an earnest effort to discern what is the will and guidance of God. This is not a subject where a congregation makes a decision based on a carefully crafted political move to gain a majority vote. Rather it should be a decision where all involved feel that God's Spirit has given them the direction they have requested.

BIBLIOGRAPHY ON HOMOSEXUALITY

Adams, H.E. & Sturgis, E. T., 1977. "Status of behavioral reorientation techniques in the modification of homosexuallity: A review." *Psychological Bulletin*, 84, pp. 1171-1188.

American Psychologist, 2000. "Guidelines for Psychotherapy With Lesbian, Gay, and Bisexual Clients, Vol.55, No.12, pp. 1440-1451.

Anderson, Wendell and Nancy Anderson, 1998. *On Eagle's Wings: Wives Manual and Family Manual.* Video series: 1. Theories Regarding Origins: What Goes Wrong? 2.Hope For Change: Is There a Way Out? 3. Biblical Morality: What Does the Bible Say? 4. Responding to the Gay Person. 5. Can Homosexuality Be Prevented? Eagles Wings Ministry, P.O. Box 11246, Minneapolis, MN 55411.

Arkes, Hadley, 1998. *Making Sense of Homosexuality.* Claremont, California: Claremont Institute.

Bailey, Michael, 1999. "Homosexuality and mental illness," Article in the series entitled, "Sexual Orientation and Suicidality." *Archives of General Psychiatry* Oct., Vol.56, No.10, pp.867-888.

Ballew, John R., 1985. *A Call For Dialog.* Paper published by Lutherans Concerned/North America. P.O.Box 10461, Fort Dearborn Station, Chicago, IL 60610-0461.

Bayer, R., 1981. *Homosexuality and American Psychiatry: The Politics of Diagnosis.* New York: Basic Books, pp.3-4.

Bell, A. and Weinberg, M., 1978. *Homosexualities: A Study of Diversity among Men and Women.* New York: Simon and Schuster.

Bieber, Irving, 1987. "On arriving at the American Psychiatric Association Decision on homosexuality." *Scientific Controversies: Case Studies in the Resolution and Closure of Disputes in Science and Technology* edited by H. Tristam Engelhardt and Arthur Caplan, Cambridge, Massachusetts: University Press.

Benson, Peter L., 1997. *All Kids Are Our Kids.* San Francisco: Jossey–Bass Publishers, pp. 7, 264

Birk, L., 1974. "Group psychotherapy for men who are homosexual." *Journal of Sex and Marital Therapy* 1, pp. 29-52.

Bishops of The Evangelical Lutheran Church in America, 1996. "An open letter," March 22, 1996.

Boswell, John, 1980. *Christianity, Social Tolerance, and Homosexuality: Gay People in Western Europe from the Beginning of the Christian Era to the Fourteenth Century* Chicago and London: The University of Chicago Press.

Brelis, Matthew, 1999. "Gay gene." *The Boston Globe,* February 7.

Browning, Frank 1994. *The Culture of Desire: Paradox and Perversity in Gay Lives Today* New York: Vintage Books

Byne, William and Parsons, Bruce, 1999. "Human sexual orientation." *Homosexuality and American Public Life.* Dallas: Spencer Publishing Co., pp.228-239.

Byrd, A. Dean and Richard W. Potts, 1998. "Towards the Ethical and Effective Treatment of Homosexuality." University of Utah (Pending publication), p.16.

Cammeron, P., W. L. Playfair, and S. Wellum, 1994. "Longevity of Homosexuals." *Omega,* Vol. 29, pp.249-272.

Center for Disease Control and Prevention (1997) Table 55, "Acquired immunodeficiency syndrome (AIDS) cases, according to race, Hispanic origin, sex, and transmission category," p. 205.

Chauncey, George (1994) *Gay New York.* New York: HarperCollins, Basic Books Division, pp.1, 5, 9.

Clippinger, J. A., 1974. "Homosexuality can be cured." *Journal of Behavior Technology, Methods and Therapy* vol. 20, pp.15-28.

Cohen, Richard A., 1994. "Healing Homosexuality." *New Techniques in the Treatment of Homosexuality,* Collected Papers from the NARTH Annual Spring Conference, p. 21.

Cohen, Richard. 2000. *Coming Out Straight: Understanding and Healing Homosexuality* Winchester, Va.: Oakhill Press.

Cory, Donald Webster, 1961. "Homosexuality." *The Encyclopedia of Sexual Behavior* Vol. I, New York: Hawthorn Books, p. 486.

Consiglio, W. E., 1999. "When homosexuality hits home: Working with the focal family member." *New Techniques in the Treatment of Homosexuality,* Collected papers from the Narth Annual Spring Conference., May, 1994.

Dannecker, Martin, 1991. *Der Homosexuelle Mann inn Zeichen von AIDS.* Hamburg, Germany: Klein Verlag.

Dickson, Gregory L., 1999. "Mothers of homosexuals: a study." *NARTH Bulletin* vol. 7, no.1, April. National Association for Research and Therapy of Homosexuality, pp. 7-8, 34.

Donaldson, Steven, 1998. "Sexual-Reorientation: ACA Prohibits Publication." *NARTH Bulletin,* December, Vol.6, No.3, p. 8.

Duluth News Tribune, 1999. News of Note, p. 4B.

Epstein, Louis M., 1948. *Sex Laws and Customs of Judaism.* New York: loch Publishing Co. Inc.

Finkelhor, D., 1981. "The Sexual Abuse of Boys," *Victimology: An International Journal,* Vol. 6.

Fisher, Seymour and Roger Greenberg, 1996. *Freud Scientifically Reappraised: Testing the Theories and Therapy.* New York: John Wiley and Sons.

Ford, C .S. and F. A. Beach, 1951. *Patterns of Sexual Behavior.* New York: Harper and Row.

Gagnon, Robert A.J., 2001. *The Bible and Homosexual Practice:Texts and Hermeneutics* Nashville: Abingdon Press.

Garnet, Linda, et al, 1991. "Issues in Psychotherapy With Lesbians and Gay Men." *American Psychologist*, September, pp. 964-972.

Gillespie, Thomas W., 1996. Transcript of speech given at *Presbyterians for Renewal* in Albuquerque, July 3.

Glasner, Samuel, 1961. "Judaism and Sex." *The Encyclopedia of Sexual Behavior,* Vol.II, p. 579. New York: Hawthorn Books: New York.

Gomes, Peter J., 1996. *The Good Book: Reading the Bible With the Mind and Heart.* New York: William Morrow and Company.

Goode, Erica, 1999. "Booklet on Gays Sent to Schools." *New York Times,* November 11, published in the *St. Paul Pioneer Press*, pp.1, 8A.

Greenidge, Charles Wilton Wood, 1964. "Slavery." *Encyclopaedia Britannica,* Volume 20, pp.777-778. Chicago: William Benton, Publisher.

Grenz, Stanley, 1998. *Welcoming But Not Affirming*, Louisville: Westminister John Knox Press, pp. 153, 62, 118.

Griswold, Frank, 1998. "Frank Griswold on human sexuality." *The Source,* September 1, p.1.

Harry, J., 1982. *Gay Children Grown Up*. New York: Praeger.

Hawking, Stephen, 2001, *The Universe in a Nutshell*. New York: Bantam Books.

Hockenberry, S. L. and R. C. Billingham, 1987. "Sexual orientation and boyhood gender conformity: development of the boyhood gender and conformity scale (BOCS)." *Archives of Sexual Behavior* 16, pp. 475-487.

Ibrahim, A., 1976. "The home situation and the homosexual." *The Journal of Sex Research* 12, pp. 253-282.

Insight, 1990. "Gays are more prone to substance abuse." November, p.5

James, E.C., 1978. *Treatment of homosexuality: A reanalysis and synthesis of outcome studies*. Unpublished doctoral dissertation. Provo, Utah: Brigham Young University.

Johnson, R. L. and D. K. Shrier, 1985. "Sexual Victimization of Boys: Experience at an Adolescent Medicine Clinic." *Journal of Adolescent Health Care,* p. 6.

Jones, Clinton R., 1972. *What About Homosexuality?* Nashville: Thomas Nelson, p. 11.
—1974. *Homosexuality and Counseling*. Philadelphia: Fortress Press.
—1976. *Understanding Gay Relatives and Friends*. New York: Seabury Press.

Jones, Stanton, 1994. "A Constructive Relationship for Religion and Profession of Psychology: Perhaps the Boldest Model Yet." *American Psychologist,* March, pp.184-199.

Jones, Stanton L. & Mark A, Yarhouse, *Homosexuality: The Use of Scientific Research in the Church's Moral Debate* . Downers Grove, Il.: InterVarsity Press.

Judson, F. N., 1984. "Sexually Transmitted Viral Hepatatis and Enteric Pathogens." *Urology Clinics of North America* 11, no.1, February, pp.177-85.

Justin, Neal, 2000. "Sex smothers the issues in 'Queer as Folk.'" *Minneapolis Star Tribune,* Friday, December 1, pp. E1, 2.

Kiefer, Otto, 1934. *Sexual Life in Ancient Rome,* London: Routledge.

Kuenning, Paul P., 1988. *Rise and Fall of American Lutheran Pietism*. Macon, Georgia: Mercer University Press.

La Barbera, Peter, 2000. "Dirkhising bondage/torture like those in homosexual sadistic publications." *Lambda Report*, Vol.7, No.1, pp. 1-4.

Laumann, Edward O., John H. Gagnon, Robert T. Michael, and Stuart Michaels, 1994. *The Social Organization of Sexuality: Sexual Practices in the United States.* Chicago: University of Chicago Press, pp. 297, 537.

LeVay, Simon, 1995. *Queer Science*. Cambridge, Massachusetts: MIT Press.

Licht, Hans, 1925. *Liebe und Ehe in Griechenland*. Berlin: Paul Aretz.

Louganis, Greg, 1995. *Breaking the Surface*. New York: Random House.

Luther, Martin, 1909. "A treatise on Christian liberty." *Works of Martin Luther,* Vol.II, First Edition. Minneapolis: The Luther Press, p.189.

—"Answer to the superchristian, superspiritual, and super learned book of goat Emser." *Works of Martin Luther,* Vol.III, p.350.

—"The Babylonian Captivity of the Church," *Works of Martin Luther,* Vol.II

MacIntosh, H., 1994. "Report on survey of 285 psychoanalysts." *Journal of the American Psychoanalytic Association,* p. 274.

Marcus, Eric, 1999. *Is It A Choice?* San Francisco: HarperSanFrancisco.

McGeary, Johanna, 2001. "Death Stalks a Continent." *TIME: The Weekly Newsmagazine,* February 12, Vol.157, No.6., pp.36-53.

McNeill, John J., 1988. *Taking a Chance on God: Liberating Theology for Gays, Lesbians, and Their Lovers, Families, and Friends.* Boston: Beacon Press, p.22

McWhirter, D. and Mattison, A., 1984. *The Male Couple: How Relationships Develop.* Englewood Cliffs, New Jersey: Prentice Hall.

Medinger, Alan P., 1994. "Softball Therapy." *New Techniques in the Treatment of Homosexuality* (Collected Papers from the NARTH Annual Spring Conference).

Michael, Robert T., John H. Gagnon, Edward O. Laumann, and Gina Kolata, 1994. *Sex in America: A Definitve Survey.* Boston: Little, Brown and Company.

Money, John, 1988. *Gay, Straight, and In-Between.* New York: Oxford University Press, pp.10, 50, 55-56.

Morin, S., 1977. "Heterosexual bias in psychological research on lesbianism and male homosexuality." *American Psychologist* 32, pp.629-637.

NARTH Bulletin, 1998. National Association for Research and Therapy of Homosexuality. "Prevention of Male Homosexuality" Fact Sheet. Vol.6, No.3, December.

NARTH Bulletin, 2000. National Association for Research and Therapy of Homosexuality. "The Causes of Male Homosexuality" Fact Sheet. Vol.8., No.1, April.

National Center for Health Statistics, 1999. "Selected notifiable disease rates, according to disease." *Health,* United States, With Health and Aging Chart Books, Hyattsville, Maryland.

News Note, 1999. *Duluth News-Tribune.* Saturday, November 6, p.4B.

News Reporter 2001. *Monitor on Psychology*—publication of American Psychological Association, Dec., p.20

Nicolosi, Joseph, 1997. *Reparative Therapy of Male Homosexuality.* Northvale, New Jersey: Jason Aronson, pp.11, 25, 62.

—1999. "Prevention of male homosexuality."

NARTH FACT SHEET. Ventura, California: Association of Research and Therapy of Homosexuality, p.4.

—2000. "Dr. Laura" interviews Psychiatric Association's Robert Spitzer, *NARTH,* Vol.8, No.1, p. 26.

—2000. Letter sent to all NARTH members in April

—1994. "The homosexually oriented man's relationship to women." *New Techniques in the Treatment of Homosexuality.* Collected papers from the NARTH Annual Spring Conferecnce. National Association for Research and Therapy of Homosexuality, p. 68.

—1999. Personal corresponce.

—2000. "NARTH signs on to full-page newspaper ad." NARTH BULLETIN, Vol. 8, No. 2, p. 3.

—2000. *NARTH BULLETIN,*

—2000. "Prevention of male homosexuality." Lecture given at North Heights Lutheran Church, August 5. Quotes taken from *Notes* in program guide.

Niebuhr, H. Richard, 1951. *Christ and Culture.* New York: Harper & Brothers, p.83.

Pannenberg, Wolfhart, 1996. "You Shall Not Lie With a Male." *Lutheran Forum,* Vol. 30, No.1, February, p. 29.

Perloff, Robert, 2002, Correspondence to NARTH , February 15, 2002.

Pharr, Suzanne, 1988. *Homophobia: A Weapon of Sexism.* Inverness, California: Chardon Press, p.45.

Pollack, M., 1985. "Male homosexuality." *Western Sexuality: Practice and Precept in Past and Present Times,* ed. P. Aries and A. Bejin, pp.40-61. New York: Basil Blackwell.

Position Paper, 1998. "Living with tensions," *Council of the Evangelical Church in Germany.* On the issue of Homosexuality and the Church, Herrenhauser Strabe, Hannover, Germany pp. 9, 15.

Prager, D., 1990. "Judaism, Homosexuality, and Civilization." *Ultimate Issues* 6, no.2, p. 2.

Psychiatric News, 1999. "American Psychiatric Association Maintains Reparative Therapy Not Effective." *Psychiatric News Main Frame.* Tuesday, December 14, www.psch.org

Remafedi, G., M. Resnick, R. Blum, and L. Harris. "Demography of sexual orientation in adolescents." *Pediatrics,* vol.89, April, pp. 714-21.

Riehl, Carolyn, 1998. *Pulpit Fiction: The gifts and burdens of Gay Men and Lesbians Serving in the Ordained Ministry.* Unpublished Paper, pp. 4-5.

Rogers, C., H. Roback, E. Mckee, and D. Calhoun, 1976. "Group psychotherapy with homosexuals: A review." *International Journal of Group Psychotherapy,* 26, pp. 3-27.

Rosenberg, Samuel, 2000. News Notes, *NARTH Bulletin,* Vol. 8, p. 7.

Rotello, Gabriel, 1998. "This is Sexual Ecology," *The Harvard Gay and Lesbian Review,* Spring, Volume Five, No. 2, p. 24.

Sadock, Benjamin and Virginia Sadock, editors, 2000. *Kaplan and Sadock's Comprehensive Textbook of Psychiatry.* Philadelphia: Lippincott Williams & Wilkins, pp.1608-9, 1628, 1627.

Satcher, David, 2001. "The Surgeon General's Call to Action to Promote Sexual Health and Responsible Sexual Behavior" A Letter from the U.S. Department of Health and Human Services, June, pp.1-33.

Satinover, Jeffrey, 1996. *Homosexuality and the Politics of Truth.* Grand Rapids, Michigan: Baker Books, pp.186, 77, 142, 137, 223.

Scharmann, Brent, 1999. Luncheon speech. *NARTH BULLETIN,* Volume 7, Number 3, p. 16.

Schmierer, Don, 1998. *An Ounce of Prevention: Preventing the Homosexual Condition in Today's Youth.* Nashville: Word Publishing.

Socarides, C. W., 1992. "Sexual Politics and Scientific Logic: The Issue of Homosexuality." *The Journal of Psychohistory,* 10, no. 3, p. 308.

Source, The, 1998. "Frank Griswold on Human Sexuality." 9/1, p. 1.

Spitzer, R. L., 1973. "A Proposal About Homosexuality and the APA Nomenclature: Homosexuality as an Irregular Form of Sexual Behavior and Sexual Orientation Disturbance as a Psychiatric Disorder." *Am. J. Psychiatry,* 130, pp. 1207-1216.

Staller, Craig S., 2001. "Something Personal." *Christian Century,* January 17.

Stein, Terry, 2000. "Homosexuality and Homosexual Behavior." *Kaplan & Sadock's Comprehensive Textbook of Psychiatry.* Philadelphia: Lippincott Williams & Wilkins, pp. 1615-16, 1608, 1612-14.

Strommen, Merton P., editor, 1971. *Research on Religious Development: A Comprehensive Handbook.* New York: Hawthorn Books Inc.

—1993. *Five Cries of Youth* (2nd revised edition). San Francisco: Harper SanFrancisco, pp. 90-92.

Strommen, Merton P., Milo L. Brekke, Ralph C. Underwager, Art L. Johnson, 1972. *A Study of Generations.* Minneapolis: Augsburg Publishing House, pp.132-133.

Strommen, Merton P. and Richard Hardel, 2000. *Passing on the Faith: A Radical New Model for Youth and Family Ministry.* Winona, Minnesota: St. Mary's Press.

Sullivan, Andrew, 1998. *Love Undetectable: Notes on Friendship, Love and Survival.* New York: Random House.

Throckmorton, Warren, 1998. "Attempts to Modify Sexual Orientation: A Review of Outcome Literature and Ethical Issues." *The Journal of Mental Health Counseling,* Vol.20, pp. 283-304.

Throckmorton, Warren, "Empirical Findings Concerning Ex-Gays: Initial Findings Concerning the Change Process."

Wardle, Lynn D., 2000. "When Dissent Is Stifled: The Same-Sex Marriage and Right-to-Treatment Debates." *NARTH Bulletin,* August, Vol. 8, No. 2, p. 26.

Wells, Roland J., 2002. "Toward a Biblical , Pastoral Teaching on Homosexuality" Unpublished paper. Minneapolis, Minn.

Whelan, Elizabeth M., 1989. "Needless offenses in AIDS education." *New York Times,* p. 23A.

White, Mel, 1994. *Stranger at the Gate.* New York: Simon & Schuster, p.254.

—2000. Letter to the Editor. *Christian Century,* June 21-28, p. 699.

Whitehead, Neil E. and Briar K. Whitehead, 1999. *My Genes Made Me Do It! A Scientific Look at Sexual Orientation.* Huntington House Publishers.

—1999. Comments made to the editor of *NARTH BULLETIN,* December issue, Volume 7, No. 3, p. 23.

Whitham, F. L., 1977. "Childhood indicators of male homosexuality." *Archives of Sexual Behavior* 6, pp. 89-96.

Wink, Walter, editor, 1999. *Homosexuality and Christian Faith.* Minneapolis: Fortress Press, pp. 36-37, 46-47.

Yancey, Phillip, 1997. *What's So Amazing About Grace?* Grand Rapids, Michigan: Zondervan Publishing House, p. 170.

Yarhouse, M. A., 1998. "When clients seek treatment for same-sex attraction: ethical issues in the 'Right to Choose' debate." *Psychotherapy,* Vol. 35, No.2, Summer, pp. 248-259.